Praise for *Leadership and Self-Deception*

"Extraordinary . . . Five Stars."
— *Business Ethics*

"This is the most profound and practical business book I have ever read!
Everyone I have recommended this book to has been challenged
intellectually and also touched emotionally. It is a must-read that I will
give to my kids to read before they begin their careers."
— Tom A. Didonato, Vice President, Human Resources, Heinz North
America

"I love this book. It identifies the central issue in all organizational
performance. Like truth itself, this book reveals more with each re-
examination. I highly recommend it."
— Doug Hauth, Sales Vice President, Lucent Technologies

"Imagine working in an organization where the aim of your colleagues is
to help you achieve your results. I could not believe it possible. After
reading this book I just had to bring Arbinger to the UK to teach our
people. What an experience! We are all better people for it. This book
touches the very foundation of culture, teamwork, and performance. It's a
must for everyone."
— Mark Ashworth, President and CEO, Butcher's Pet Care, UK

"It's rare to find a business book that is good enough to recommend to
your boss, your work team, and your friends. The concepts in this book
have transformed both the way I work and the way I live."
— Robert W. Edwards, Managing Director, Worldwide Services,
FedEx

"After decades of executive leadership in senior management positions,
I've finally found in Arbinger what I consider to be the best means of
improving every measure of success. From boosting the bottom line to
increasing personal joy, this book shows the way."
— Bruce L. Christensen, Former President and CEO, PBS

"This astonishing book is a MUST read for every executive or personal
and professional coach."
— Laura Whitworth, coauthor of *Co-Active Coaching*, and
Cofounder, The Coaches Training Institute

"While reading, I reviewed my life, and, sure enough, what successes there were in it were based on Arbinger's principles. This book is a tool that could transform and elevate the way government functions!"
— Mark W. Cannon, Former Administrative Assistant to the Chief Justice of the United States, and Staff Director, Commission on the Bicentennial of the U.S. Constitution

"Simple . . . clear . . . powerful. With many years of experience in leadership, organizational development, and training I was surprised to find something strike me with such impact."
— Janet Steinwedel, Director, Leadership and Employee Development, Delaware Investments

"Arbinger has provided training for Anasazi for more than 10 years. The material in this book is an integral part of the incredible successes we experience with at-risk youth and their parents. Thank you, Arbinger!"
— Michael J. Merchant, CEO, Anasazi Foundation

"The concepts in this book are powerful. They are fundamental to success whether on the playing field, in the office, or perhaps most importantly, at home. Read this book and you'll see what I mean."
— Steve Young, two-time NFL Most Valuable Player

"Once I started I couldn't put it down .... [it's] nothing short of a transformational book disguised as a business manager's guide."
— A Reader from Springfield, Massachusetts, online review

"The principles in the book are so powerful that you cannot help referring to them constantly in your every day dealings with other people . . . . [The] truths in it have lasting effect, and definitively change the way you view life."
— A Reader from Berkeley, California, online review

"WOW! My world has changed because of this book."
— A Reader from Missoula, Montana, online review

"My freshman roommate once told me there are some books so precious to you that you are amazed you can just buy them at the bookstore for $20 like everyone else. This is one of those books . . . . All in all, this one makes it onto my list of my favorite books ever written."
— A Reader from Austin, Texas, online review

"I love this book! It completely changed the way I view work. Makes me wonder how much time and energy I wasted working in the box!"
  —A Reader from Salt Lake City, Utah, online review

"Profound! Just what I have always looked for in a 'leadership' book but could never find . . . . No part of my life has been untouched."
  —A Reader from Richmond, Virginia, online review

"I believe [this] will be one of the most important books of the decade, and believe that the concepts it teaches have the strength and truth in them to transform lives."
  —A Reader from Northern California, online review

"I wish I'd read [this book] ten years ago; it's become a favorite among my closest friends and colleagues. It's a cultural prerequisite for creating both great companies and superior family dynamics."
  —A Reader from Fort Lauderdale, Florida, online review

"Those who think highly of *Who Moved My Cheese?* will find this book especially valuable . . . . I urge you to obtain a copy immediately and read it, then re-read it. It can be valuable to your understanding of why so many people create their own problems, are unable and/or unwilling to see that they are creating their own problems, and then resist any attempts by others to help them stop creating those problems."
  —A Reader from Dallas, Texas, online review

"Upon finishing this book, I felt like Ebeneezer Scrooge on Christmas morning."
  —A Reader From Victoria, BC, Canada, online review

"This book will change your life . . . . It is an easy read that you will fly through in a matter of hours. Then you will read it again! Buy this book and pass it on to everyone that you know, especially those you work with!"
  —A Reader from Wichita, Kansas, online review

LEADERSHIP
and SELF-
DECEPTION

Getting out of the Box

The Arbinger Institute

BERRETT-KOEHLER PUBLISHERS, INC.
San Francisco

Berrett-Koehler Publishers, Inc.
235 Montgomery Street, Suite 650
San Francisco, CA 94104-2916
Tel: (415) 288-0260   Fax: (415) 362-2512   www.bkconnection.com

ORDERING INFORMATION

Quantity sales. Special discounts are available on quantity purchases by
corporations, associations, and others. For details, contact the "Special
Sales Department" at the Berrett-Koehler address above.

Individual sales. Berrett-Koehler publications are available through most
bookstores. They can also be ordered direct from Berrett-Koehler: Tel:
(800) 929-2929; Fax: (802) 864-7626; www.bkconnection.com

Orders for college textbook/course adoption use. Please contact Berrett-
Koehler: Tel: (800) 929-2929; Fax: (802) 864-7626.

Orders by U.S. trade bookstores and wholesalers. Please contact
Publishers Group West, 1700 Fourth Street, Berkeley, CA 94710.
Tel: (510) 528-1444; Fax: (510) 528-3444.

Berrett-Koehler and the BK logo are registered trademarks of Berrett-
Koehler Publishers, Inc.

Printed in the United States of America

Berrett-Koehler books are printed on long-lasting acid-free paper. When it
is available, we choose paper that has been manufactured by environmen-
tally responsible processes. These may include using trees grown in sus-
tainable forests, incorporating recycled paper, minimizing chlorine in
bleaching, or recycling the energy produced at the paper mill.

Library of Congress Cataloging-in-Publication Data

Leadership and self-deception: getting out of the box / by the Arbinger
     Institute.
       p.   cm.
     Includes index.
     ISBN 1-57675-174-0 (pbk.)
        1. Leadership. 2. Self-deception. I. Arbinger Institute.
     HD57.7 .L4315 2000
     658.4'092—dc21   99-086442

First Hardcover Edition 2000, First Paperback Edition 2002

07 06 05   20 19 18 17

Copyediting and proofreading: PeopleSpeak
Interior design and production: Marin Bookworks
Cover design: Meyer & Leichty

"It is in the darkness of their eyes that men get lost."
—Black Elk

Contents

Preface

For too long, the issue of self-deception has been the realm of deep-thinking philosophers, academics, and scholars working on the central questions of the human sciences. The public remains generally unaware of the issue. That would be fine except that self-deception is so pervasive it touches every aspect of life. "Touches" is perhaps too gentle a word to describe its influence. Self-deception actually *determines* one's experience in every aspect of life. The extent to which it does that, and in particular the extent to which it is the central issue in leadership, is the subject of this book.

To give you an idea of what's at stake, consider the following analogy. An infant is learning to crawl. She begins by pushing herself backward around the house. Backing herself around, she gets lodged beneath the furniture. There she thrashes about—crying and banging her little head against the sides and undersides of the pieces. She is stuck and hates it. So she does the only thing she can think of to get herself out—she pushes even harder, which only worsens her problem. She's more stuck than ever.

If this infant could talk, she would blame the furniture for her troubles. She, after all, is doing everything she can think of. The problem couldn't be *hers*. But of course, the problem *is* hers, even though she can't see it. While it's true she's doing everything she can think of, the problem is precisely that *she can't see how she's the problem*. Having the problem she has, nothing she can think of will be a solution.

Self-deception is like this. It blinds us to the true cause of problems, and once blind, all the "solutions" we can think of will actually make matters worse. That's why self-deception is so central to leadership—because leadership is about making matters better. To the extent we are self-deceived, our leadership is undermined at every turn—and not because of the furniture.

We have written this book to educate people about this most central of problems—a problem that has been the exclusive terrain of scholars for far too long. But this book is about more than the problem. There is a solution to self-deception as well.

Our experience in teaching about self-deception and its solution is that people find this knowledge liberating. It sharpens vision, reduces feelings of conflict, enlivens the desire for teamwork, redoubles accountability, magnifies the capacity to achieve results, and deepens satisfaction and happiness. We hope that this introduction to the self-deception problem and solution will give people new leverage in all of these areas. In organizations as varied as commercial ventures, neighborhoods, and families, what is needed most is people not just with influence but with influence for good.

A Note about the Book

Although based on actual experiences in our work with organizations, no character or organization described in this book represents any specific person or organization. However, the information that appears about Ignaz Semmelweis is an actual historical account drawn from the book *Childbed Fever: A Scientific Biography of Ignaz Semmelweis*, by K. Codell Carter and Barbara R. Carter (Westport, Conn.: Greenwood Press, 1994).

PART I

Self-Deception
and the "Box"

1   *Bud*

It was two months ago to the day that I first entered the secluded campus-style headquarters of Zagrum Company to interview for a senior management position. I'd been watching the company for more than a decade from my perch at one of its competitors and had tired of finishing second. After eight interviews and a three-week period of silence and self-doubt, I was hired to lead one of Zagrum's product lines.

I was about to be introduced to a senior management ritual peculiar to Zagrum—a day-long, one-on-one meeting with the executive vice president, Bud Jefferson. Bud was right-hand man to Zagrum's president, Kate Stenarude. And due to a shift within the executive team, he was about to become my new boss.

I had tried to find out what this meeting was all about, but my colleagues' explanations confused me. They mentioned a discovery that solves "people problems," how no one really focuses on results, and that something about the "Bud Meeting," as it was called, and strategies that evidently follow from it, is key to Zagrum's incredible success. I had no idea what they were talking about, but I was eager to meet, and impress, my new boss.

I knew Bud by reputation only. He had been present at a product rollout conference I attended but had taken no active part. He was a youngish-looking 50-year-old combination of odd-fitting characteristics: a wealthy man who drove around in an economy car without hubcaps; a near high-school dropout who graduated with law and business degrees, summa cum laude, from Harvard; a connoisseur of the arts who was hooked on the Beatles. Despite his apparent contradictions, and perhaps partly because of them, Bud was revered as something of an icon in the company—like Zagrum, mysterious yet open, driven yet humane, polished yet real. He was universally admired, if wondered about, in the company.

It took 10 minutes on foot to cover the distance from my office in Building 8 to the lobby of the Central Building. The pathway—one of 23 connecting Zagrum's 10 buildings—meandered beneath oak and maple canopies along the banks of Kate's Creek, a postcard-perfect manmade stream that was the brainchild of Kate Stenarude and named after her by the employees.

As I scaled the Central Building's hanging steel stairway up to the third floor, I reviewed my performance during my month at Zagrum: I was always among the earliest to arrive and latest to leave. I felt that I was focused and didn't let outside matters interfere with my objectives. Although my wife often complained of it, I was making a point to outwork and outshine every coworker who might compete for promotions in the coming years. I had nothing to be ashamed of. I was ready to meet Bud Jefferson.

Arriving in the main lobby of the third floor, I was greeted by Bud's secretary, Maria. "You must be Tom Callum," she said with enthusiasm.

"Yes, thank you. I have an appointment with Bud for 9:00," I said.

"Yes. Bud asked me to have you wait for him in the Eastview Room. He should be with you in about five minutes." Maria escorted me down the hall and left me to myself in a large conference room, where from the long bank of windows I admired the views of the campus between the leaves of the green Connecticut wood. A minute or so later there was a brisk knock on the door and in walked Bud.

"Hello, Tom. Thanks for coming," he said with a big smile as he offered me his hand. "Please, sit down. Can I get something for you to drink? Coffee, juice?"

"No, thank you," I replied, "I've had plenty already this morning."

I settled in the black leather chair nearest me, my back to the window, and waited for Bud as he poured himself some water out of the pitcher in the serving area in the corner. He walked back with his water, bringing the pitcher and an extra glass with him. He set them on the table between us. "Sometimes things can get pretty hot in here. We have a lot to do this morning. Please, feel free whenever you'd like."

"Thanks," I stammered. I was grateful for the gesture but more unsure than ever what this was all about.

"Tom," said Bud abruptly, "I've asked you to come today for one reason—an important reason."

"Okay," I said evenly, trying to mask the anxiety I was feeling.

"You have a problem—a problem you're going to have to solve if you're going to make it at Zagrum."

I felt as if I'd been kicked in the stomach. I groped for some appropriate word or sound, but my mind was racing and words failed me. I was immediately conscious of the pounding of my heart and the sensation of blood draining from my face.

As successful as I had been in my career, one of my hidden weaknesses was that I was too easily knocked off balance. I had learned to compensate by training the muscles in my face and eyes to relax so that no sudden twitch would betray my alarm. And now, it was as if my face instinctively knew

5

that it had to detach itself from my heart or I would be found out to be the same cowering third-grader who broke into an anxious sweat, hoping for a "well done" sticker, every time Mrs. Lee passed back the homework.

Finally I managed to say, "A problem? What do you mean?"

"Do you really want to know?" asked Bud.

"I'm not sure. I guess I need to from the sound of it."

"Yes," Bud agreed, "you do."

2 A Problem

"You have a problem," Bud continued. "The people at work know it; your spouse knows it; your mother-in-law knows it. I bet even your neighbors know it." He was smiling warmly. "The problem is that *you* don't know it."

I found myself speechless. How could I know I had a problem if I didn't even know what the problem was?

"I'm afraid I don't know what you mean. Are you saying that I . . . that I. . . ." I had *no idea* what he was talking about.

"Well," he said in a way that made me think he was enjoying this, "think about these examples for starters.

"Remember the time you had a chance to fill the car with gas before your wife took it, but then you decided she could fill it just as easily as you, so you took the car home empty?"

How did he know about that? I wondered.

"Or the time you promised the kids a trip to the ballpark but backed out at the last minute, on some feeble excuse, because something more appealing had come up?"

How did he know about that?

"Or the time, under similar circumstances, you took the kids to the ball game anyway but made them feel guilty for it?"

Uh-oh.

"Or the time, when reading to your toddler, you cheated him by turning more than one page at a time because you were impatient and 'he wouldn't notice anyway'?"

Yeah, but he didn't *notice.*

"Or the time you parked in a Handicapped Only parking zone and then faked a limp so people wouldn't think you were a total jerk?"

Hah! I've never done that.

"Or the time you did the same thing but ran from the car with apparent purpose to show that your errand was so important that you just *had* to park there?"

Well, I have to admit I have done that.

"Or the time, driving at night, the driver of a car close behind you kept his brights on, and you let him pass so you could do the same thing back to him?"

So?

"And think of your style at work," he continued, now on a roll. "Do you sometimes demean others? Are you sometimes punishing and disdainful toward the people around you, scornful of their laziness and incompetence?"

"I guess that's true part of the time," I muttered. I had to admit it; he seemed to know. "But—"

"Or do you more often try to do the acceptable thing?" he interrupted. "Do you indulge the people who report to you with kindness and all the other 'soft stuff' you can think of in order to get them to do what you want—even though you still feel basically scornful toward them?"

This was hitting below the belt. "I work hard at treating my people right," I protested.

"I'm sure you do," he said. "But let me ask you a question. How do you feel when you're 'treating them right,' as you say? Is it any different from the way you feel when you're being punishing and scornful toward people? Deep down, is there any difference?"

"I'm not sure I know what you mean," I replied, stalling for time.

"I mean this: Do you feel you have to 'put up' with people? Do you feel—honestly, now—that you have to work pretty hard to succeed as a manager when you're stuck with the kind of people you're stuck with?"

"Stuck?" I asked, still stalling.

"Think about it. You know what I mean," he said, still smiling.

I thought frantically. There was no escape. Finally, I replied: "Well, I guess it's true. I do think a lot of people are lazy and incompetent. But what am I supposed to do? Telling them doesn't usually help. So I try to get them going in other ways. Some I cajole, others I try to motivate, others I outsmart, and so on. And I try to smile a lot. I'm kind of proud of how I handle myself, actually."

Bud smiled kindly. "I understand. But when we're finished, you won't be so proud of it. What you're doing is often wrong."

I was incredulous. "How can it be wrong to treat people right?"

"But you're *not* treating them right. That's the problem. And you're doing more damage than you know."

"What do you mean? You're going to have to explain that to me." Angry now, as well as befuddled, I wanted to know what he was up to.

"I'll be happy to explain it to you," he said calmly. "I can help you learn what your problem is — *and* what to do about it. That's why we're meeting." He paused and then added, "I can help you because I have the same problem."

Bud rose from his chair — slowly, even solemnly — and began pacing the length of the table. "To begin with, you need to know about a problem at the heart of the human sciences."

3   *Self-Deception*

"You have kids, don't you, Tom?"

I was grateful for the simple question and felt the life come back to my face. "Why, yes, one actually. His name is Todd. He's 16."

"You remember how you felt when he was born—how it seemed to change your perspective on life?" Bud asked.

It had been a long while since I considered those early thoughts surrounding Todd's birth. So much had happened since then that those memories had been swept downstream by a decade of bitter words and memories. Todd had been diagnosed as having attention deficit disorder (ADD), and it was impossible for me to think of Todd without feeling a disturbance in my soul. He was nothing but trouble and had been for years. But Bud's question called me back to a sweeter time. "Yes, I remember," I began pensively. "I remember holding him close, pondering my hope for his life—feeling inadequate, even overwhelmed, but at the same time grateful." The memory lessened for a moment the pain I felt in the present.

"That was the way it was for me too," Bud said, nodding his head knowingly. "I want to tell you a story that began with the birth of *my* first child. His name is David.

"I was a young lawyer at the time, working long hours at one of the most prestigious firms in the country. One of the deals I worked on was a major financing project that involved about 30 banks worldwide. Our client was the lead lender on the deal.

"It was a complicated project involving many lawyers. In our firm alone, there were eight attorneys assigned to it from four different offices worldwide. I was the second most junior member of the team and had chief responsibility for the drafting of 50 or so agreements that sat underneath the major lending contract. It was a big, sexy deal involving international travel, numbers with lots of zeros, and high-profile characters.

"A week after I'd been assigned to the project, Nancy and I found out she was pregnant. It was a marvelous time for us. David was born some eight months later, on December 16. Before the birth I worked hard to wrap up or assign my projects so that I could take three weeks off with our new baby. I don't think I've ever been happier in my life.

"But then came a phone call. It was December 29. The lead partner on the deal was calling me. I was needed at an 'all-hands' meeting in San Francisco.

"'How long?' I asked.

"'Until the deal closes—could be three weeks, could be three months. We're here until it's done,' he said.

"I was crushed. The thought of leaving Nancy and David alone in our Alexandria, Virginia, home left me desperately sad. It took me two days to wrap up my affairs in D.C. before I reluctantly boarded a plane for San Francisco. I left my young family at the curb at what used to be called National Airport. With a photo album under my arm, I tore myself away from them and turned through the doors of the terminal.

"By the time I arrived at our San Francisco offices, I was the last one in on the deal. Even the guy from our London office beat me. I settled into the last remaining guest office— an office on the 21st floor. The deal headquarters, and everyone else, was on floor 25.

11

"I hunkered down and got to work. Most of the action was on 25—meetings, negotiations among all the parties, everything. But I was alone on 21—alone with my work and my photo album, which sat opened on my desk.

"I worked from 7:00 A.M. till after 1:00 A.M. every day. Three times a day I would go down to the deli in the lobby and purchase a bagel, a sandwich, or a salad. Then I'd go back up to 21 and eat while poring over the documents.

"If you had asked me at the time what my objective was, I would have told you that I was 'drafting the best possible documents to protect our client and close the deal,' or something to that effect. But you should know a couple of other things about my experience in San Francisco.

"All of the negotiations that were central to the documents I was working on were happening on the 25th floor. These 25th-floor negotiations should have been very important to me because every change to the deal had to be accounted for in all the documents I was drafting. But I didn't go up to 25 much.

"In fact, after 10 days of lobby deli food, I found out that food was being served around the clock in the main conference room on 25 for everyone working on the deal. I was upset that no one had told me about it. And twice during those 10 days I was chewed out for failing to incorporate some of the latest changes into my documents. No one had told me about those either! Another time I was chewed out for being hard to find. And on two occasions during that period, the lead partner asked for my opinion on issues that had never occurred to me—issues that would have occurred to me had I been thinking. They were in my area of responsibility. He shouldn't have had to do my job for me."

At this, Bud sat back down.

"Now, let me ask you a question, Tom. Just from the little bit you now know about my San Francisco experience, would you say that I was really committed to 'drafting the best possible documents to protect our client and close the deal'?"

"No, I don't think so," I said, surprised at the ease with which I was about to lampoon Bud Jefferson. "In fact, you don't seem like you were engaged in the project at all. You were preoccupied with something else."

"That's right," he agreed. "I *wasn't* engaged in it. And do you think the lead partner could tell?"

"I think after those 10 days it would have been obvious," I offered.

"He could tell well enough to chew me out a couple of times at the very least," Bud agreed. "How about this: Do you suppose he would say that I'd bought into the vision? Or that I was committed? Or that I was being maximally helpful to others on the deal?"

"No, I don't think so. By keeping yourself isolated you were putting things at risk—*his* things," I answered.

"I think you're right," Bud agreed. "I had become a problem. I wasn't engaged in the deal, wasn't committed, hadn't caught the vision, was making trouble for others, and so on. But consider this: How do you suppose I would have responded had someone accused me of not being committed or not being engaged? Do you think I would have agreed with them?"

I pondered the question. Although it should have been outwardly obvious, Bud might have had trouble seeing himself as others saw him at the time. "No. I suspect you might have felt defensive if someone had said that to you."

"You're right. Think about it: Who left behind a new baby to come to San Francisco? I did," he said, answering his own question. "And who was working 20-hour days? I was." Bud was becoming more animated. "And who was forced to work alone four floors below the others? I was. And to whom did people even forget to mention basic details like food plans? To me. So from my perspective, who was making things difficult for whom?"

"I guess you would have seen *others* as being the main cause of the trouble," I answered.

"You better believe it," he agreed. "And how about being committed, engaged, and catching the vision? Do you see that from my perspective, not only was I committed, I just might've been the most committed person on the deal? For from my perspective, no one had as many challenges to deal with as I had. And I was working hard in spite of them."

"That's right," I said, relaxing back into my chair and nodding affirmatively. "You *would* have felt that way."

"Now, think about it, Tom." Bud was standing again and began pacing the floor. "Remember the problem. I was uncommitted, disengaged, hadn't caught the vision, and was making things more difficult for others on the deal. That's all true. And that's a problem—a big problem. But there was a bigger problem—and it's this problem that you and I need to talk about."

He had my full attention.

"The bigger problem was that I couldn't *see* that I had a problem."

Bud paused for a moment, and then, leaning forward toward me, he said in a lower, even more earnest tone, "There is no solution to the problem of lack of commitment, for example, without a solution to the bigger problem—the problem that I can't *see* that I'm not committed."

I suddenly started to feel uneasy and could feel my face again sag to expressionlessness. I had been caught up in Bud's story and had forgotten that he was telling it to me for a reason. This story was for me. He must be thinking that *I* have a bigger problem. My mind was starting to race with self-worry when I heard Bud's voice again.

"Tom, there's a technical name for the insistent blindness I exhibited in San Francisco. Philosophers call it 'self-deception.' At Zagrum we have a less technical name for it— we call it 'being in the box.' In our way of talking, when we're self-deceived, we're 'in the box.'

"You're going to learn a lot more about the box, but as a starting point, think of it this way: In one sense, I was 'stuck' in my experience in San Francisco. I was stuck because I had a problem I didn't think I had—a problem I couldn't see. I could see matters only from my own closed perspective, and I was deeply resistant to any suggestion that the truth was otherwise. So I was in a box—cut off, closed up, blind. Does that make sense?"

"Sure. I get the idea," I responded, temporarily reconnecting with Bud and his story.

"There's nothing more common in organizations than self-deception," he continued. "For example, think about a person from your work experience who's a really big problem—say, someone who's been a major impediment to teamwork."

That was easy—Chuck Staehli, COO of my former employer. He was a jerk, plain and simple. He thought of no one but himself. "Yeah, I know such a guy."

"Well, here's the question: Does the person you're thinking of believe he's a problem like you believe he's a problem?"

"No. Definitely not."

"That's usually the case," he said, stopping directly across from me. "Identify someone with a problem and you'll be identifying someone who resists the suggestion that he has a problem. That's self-deception—the inability to see that one has a problem. Of all the problems in organizations, it's the most common—and the most damaging."

Bud placed his hands on the back of his chair, leaning against it. "Remember how a few minutes ago I mentioned that you needed to know something about a problem in the human sciences?"

"Yes."

"This is it. Self-deception—the box—is that problem." Bud paused. It was clear this was a point of major importance to him.

"At Zagrum, Tom, our top strategic initiative is to minimize individual and organizational self-deception. To give you an idea why it's so important to us," he said, starting again to pace, "I need to tell you about an analogous problem in medicine."

4   *The Problem beneath Other Problems*

"Have you ever heard of Ignaz Semmelweis?" he asked. (He pronounced it "Ignawtz Semelvice.")

"No, I don't think so. Is it a sickness or something?"

"No, no," Bud said with a chuckle. "But close. Semmelweis was a European doctor, an obstetrician, in the mid-1800s. He worked at Vienna's General Hospital, an important research hospital, where he tried to get to the bottom of a horrendous mortality rate among women in the maternity ward. In the section of the ward where Semmelweis practiced, the mortality rate was one in ten. Think of it. One in every ten women giving birth there died! Can you imagine?"

"I wouldn't have let my wife near the place," I said.

"You wouldn't have been alone. Vienna General had such a frightening reputation that some women actually gave birth on the street and *then* went to the hospital."

"I can't blame them," I said.

"Nor can I," Bud agreed.

"The collection of symptoms associated with these deaths," he continued, "became known as 'childbed fever.' Conventional medical science at the time called for separate treatment for each symptom. Inflammation meant excess blood was causing swelling—so they bled the patient or applied leeches. They treated fever the same way. Trouble breathing meant the air was bad—so they improved ventilation. And so on. But nothing worked. More than half the women who contracted the disease died within days.

"The terrible risk was well known. Semmelweis reported that patients were frequently seen 'kneeling and wringing their hands,' begging to be moved to a second section of the maternity ward where the mortality rate was one in fifty—still horrific, but far better than the one-in-ten rate in Semmelweis's section.

"Semmelweis gradually became obsessed with the problem—in particular with discovering why the mortality rate in one section of the maternity ward was so much higher than in the other. The only obvious difference between the sections was that Semmelweis's section was attended by doctors, while the other section was attended by midwives. He couldn't see why that would explain the difference, so he tried to equalize every other factor among the maternity patients. He standardized everything from birthing positions to ventilation and diet. He even standardized the way the laundry was done. He looked at every possibility but could find no answer. Nothing he tried made any measurable difference in the mortality rates."

"He must have been incredibly discouraged," I said.

"I'd imagine so," Bud agreed. "But then something happened. He took a four-month leave to visit another hospital, and upon his return he discovered that the death rate had fallen significantly in his section of the ward in his absence."

"Really?"

"Yes. He didn't know why, but it had definitely fallen. He dug in to find the reason. Gradually, his inquiry led him to think about the possible significance of research done by the doctors on cadavers."

"Cadavers?"

"Yes," he answered. "Remember, Vienna General was a teaching and research hospital. Many of the doctors split their time between research on cadavers and treatment of live patients. They hadn't seen any problem with that practice because there was as yet no understanding of germs. All they knew were symptoms. And in examining his own work practices compared to those who worked for him in his absence, Semmelweis discovered that the only significant difference was that he, Semmelweis, spent far more time doing research on the cadavers.

"From these observations, he developed a theory of childbed fever, a theory that became the precursor to germ theory. He concluded that 'particles' from cadavers and other diseased patients were being transmitted to healthy patients *on the hands of the physicians*. So he immediately instituted a policy requiring physicians to wash their hands thoroughly in a chlorine and lime solution before examining any patient. And you know what happened?"

I waited anxiously. "What?"

"The death rate immediately fell to one in a hundred."

"So he was right," I said, almost under my breath. "The doctors were the carriers."

"Yes. In fact, Semmelweis once sadly remarked, 'Only God knows the number of patients who went prematurely to their graves because of me.' Imagine living with *that*. The doctors were doing the best they knew how, but they were carrying a disease they knew nothing about. It caused a multitude of debilitating symptoms, all of which could be prevented by a single act once the common cause of the symptoms was discovered—what was later identified as a germ."

Bud stopped. He put his hands on the table and leaned toward me. "There is a similar germ that is spread in organizations—a germ we all carry to one extent or another, a germ that kills leadership, a germ that causes a multitude of 'people problems,' a germ that can be isolated and neutralized."

"What is it?" I asked.

"Just what we've been talking about," Bud replied. "Self-deception—'the box.' Or more precisely, self-deception is the disease. What we're going to learn about is the germ that causes it.

"What I'm suggesting, Tom, is that, like the discovery of the cause of childbed fever, the discovery of the cause of self-deception amounts to the revelation of a sort of unifying theory, an explanation that shows how the apparently disparate collection of symptoms we call 'people problems'—from problems in leadership to problems in motivation and everything in between—are all caused by the same thing. With this knowledge, people problems can be solved with an efficiency that has never been possible before. There is a clear way to attack and solve them—not one by one but in one disciplined stroke."

"That's quite a claim," I said.

"Indeed," Bud responded. "And it's quite a discovery. But I don't intend for you to take my word for it. I'm going to attempt to help you discover it for yourself. We need you to understand it because you need to make sure that the strategies that follow from it are implemented in your division."

"Okay," I said.

"To begin with," he said, "Let me tell you about one of my first experiences at Zagrum."

5   *Beneath Effective Leadership*

"After 10 years at the law firm, I left to become general counsel of Sierra Product Systems. Do you remember Sierra?" Bud asked, turning toward me.

Sierra had pioneered several of the processes that Zagrum had exploited to climb to its place at the top of the high-tech manufacturing heap. "You bet," I said. "Their technologies changed the industry. Whatever happened to them?"

"They were acquired—by Zagrum Company."

"Really? I never heard that."

"The deal was sort of complicated. But the long and short of it was that Zagrum acquired most of Sierra's useful intellectual property—patents and so on.

"That was sixteen years ago. At the time, I was COO of Sierra and came to Zagrum as part of the deal. I had no idea what I was getting into." Bud reached for his glass and took a drink. "At the time, Zagrum was a bit of a mystery. But I was introduced to the mystery of Zagrum in a hurry—in my second major meeting to be exact.

"Being intimately familiar with the key acquisitions from Sierra, I joined Zagrum as part of the executive team. In my first meeting, I was given several difficult assignments to complete before the next meeting in two weeks. It was a heavy load, learning the business and all.

"At last, on the night before the next meeting, there was only one assignment that I'd yet to complete. It seemed late, and I was tired. Given all I'd accomplished and been through to do it, this one remaining assignment seemed inconsequential. So I let it go.

"At the meeting the next day, I reported my achievements, made recommendations, and shared the important information I had gathered. I then told the group that because all my time had been taken up with these other assignments, not to mention all the obstacles I'd encountered, there was one assignment I hadn't yet completed.

"I'll never forget what happened next. Lou Herbert, who was then president of the company, turned to Kate Stenarude, who at the time occupied the position I have now, and asked *her* to take that assignment for the next meeting. The meeting then continued with others' reports. Nothing more was made of it, but I noticed that I was the only person in the group who had left something undone.

"I spent the rest of the meeting lost in my own thoughts — feeling embarrassed, feeling small, wondering if I belonged, wondering if I *wanted* to belong.

"The meeting closed, and I packed my documents into my briefcase as others chatted. I didn't feel part of the group at that moment and was quietly slipping past some of my bantering colleagues toward the door when I felt a hand on my shoulder.

"'Bud . . .'

"I turned and saw Lou smiling, gazing at me with his gentle yet penetrating eyes.

"'Would you mind if I walked with you back to your office?' he asked.

"'No, not at all,' I said, surprised that I really meant it."

Bud paused for a moment. "You don't know Lou, Tom, and probably haven't been here long enough to know the stories, but Lou Herbert is a legend. He was personally responsible for taking a mediocre, inconsequential company and making it into a juggernaut—sometimes in spite of, and sometimes even because of, his weaknesses. Everyone who worked at Zagrum during his era was fiercely loyal to him."

"I've heard a few stories, actually," I said. "And I remember from my work at Tetrix how even the top folks there seemed to admire him—Joe Alvarez in particular, the Tetrix CEO."

"Yeah, I know Joe," Bud nodded.

"Well," I continued, "he thought of Lou as the pioneer of the industry."

"He's right," Bud agreed. "Lou *was* the industry pioneer. But Joe doesn't know the extent of his pioneering. That's what *you're* going to learn," he emphasized. "Lou's been retired for 10 years now, but he still comes around a few times a month to see how we're doing. His insight is invaluable. We still keep an office for him.

"Anyway, I knew much of his legend before I joined the company, Tom. So perhaps you can understand my warring emotions after the meeting. I felt that I'd been slighted, but I was also supremely worried about Lou's opinion of me. And then he asked if he could walk me to my office! I was glad to have him walk with me but also afraid—of what, though, I didn't know.

"He asked me how my move had been, whether my family was settled and happy, and how I was enjoying the challenges at Zagrum. He was saddened to hear that Nancy was having a hard time with the move and promised to call her personally to see if there was anything he could do—a call he placed that very night.

"When we arrived at my office, before I could turn to go in, he took me by both shoulders with his strong, lean hands.

He looked straight into my eyes, a look of gentle concern written in the lines across his weathered face. 'Bud,' he said, 'we're happy to have you with us. You're a talented man and a good man. You add a lot to the team. But you won't ever let us down again, will you?'"

"He said *that*?" I asked incredulously.

"Yes."

"Nothing against Lou," I said, "but I think that was a little uncalled for given all you'd done. You can scare away a lot of people doing things like that."

"That's true," Bud agreed. "But you know something? It didn't happen that way for me. With Lou, in that moment, I wasn't offended. And in a way, I was even inspired. I found myself saying, 'No, Lou. I won't. I won't ever let you down again.'

"Now I know that sounds corny. But that's the way it was with Lou. He very rarely did things by the book. He probably violated every management principle known to man. If 100 people tried to do what Lou did to me in that meeting and afterward, only 1 in 100 could have invited my cooperation, as Lou did, rather than my resentment. By the book, it shouldn't have worked. But it worked anyway. And with Lou, it usually did. The question, Tom, is *why*—*why* did it work?"

That was a good question. "I don't know," I finally said, shrugging my shoulders. Then, almost as an afterthought, I said, "Maybe you just knew that Lou cared about you so you didn't feel as threatened in the situation as you might have otherwise."

Bud smiled and sat down again in the seat across from me. "What you just said is extremely important, Tom. Think about it—we can tell how other people *feel* about us, and it's to *that* that we respond. Let me give you another example.

"There were two people over in Building 6 a couple of years ago who were always dancing around each other, and it was creating trouble for the team. One of them came to me to talk about it and said, 'I don't know what to do here. I can't get Leon to respond and cooperate with me. It doesn't matter what I do; Leon doesn't seem to think that I have any interest in him. I go out of my way to ask about his family; I invite him to lunch; I've done everything I can think of doing, but nothing helps.'

"'I want you to consider something, Gabe,' I said to him. 'Really think about it. When you're going out of your way to do all those things for Leon so that he'll know you have an interest in him, what are you most interested in — *him* or his opinion of *you?*'

"I think Gabe was a little surprised by the question. 'Perhaps Leon thinks you're not really interested in him,' I continued, 'because you're really more interested in yourself.'

"Gabe finally understood the problem, but it was a painful moment. It was up to him, then, to figure out what to do about it, applying some of the things that you and I are going to cover today."

Bud gave me a long look, as if to read what I was thinking. "Let me give you another example," he said, "closer to home.

"One morning years ago, Nancy and I were locked in an argument. As I recall, she was upset that I hadn't cleaned the dishes the night before, and I was upset that she was so upset about it. Do you get the picture?"

"Oh yeah, I've been there," I said, thinking of the latest in the long line of tiffs I'd had with my wife, Laura, that very morning.

"After a while, Nancy and I had actually worked our ways to opposite sides of the room," Bud continued. "I was tiring of our little 'discussion,' which was making me late for work, and decided to apologize and put an end to it. I walked over to her and said, 'I'm sorry, Nancy,' and bent down to kiss her.

"Our lips met, if at all, only for a millisecond. It was the world's shortest kiss. I didn't intend it that way, but it was all either of us could muster.

"'You don't mean it,' she said quietly, as I backed slowly away. And she was right, of course—for just the reason we've been talking about. The way I really felt came through. I felt wronged, burdened, and unappreciated, and I couldn't cover it up—even with a kiss. But I remember wandering down the hall toward the garage, shaking my head and muttering to myself. Now I had more evidence of my wife's unreasonableness: she couldn't even accept an apology.

"But here's the point, Tom: Was there an apology to accept?"

"No, because you didn't really mean it, just like Nancy said."

"That's right. My words said 'I'm sorry,' but my feelings didn't, and it was the way I was feeling—revealed as it was through my voice, my gaze, my posture, my level of interest in her needs, and so on—it was *that* that she responded to."

Bud paused, and I thought of that morning with Laura: her face, a face that once radiated energy, concern, and love for life, now obscured by resignation to a deep hurt, her words tearing holes in whatever convictions I still held for our marriage. "I don't feel like I know you anymore, Tom," she had said. "And what's worse, I get the feeling most of the time that you don't really care to know *me*. It's like I weigh you down or something. I don't know the last time I felt love from you.

It's all coldness now. You just bury yourself in your work—even when you're home. And to be honest, I don't really have strong feelings for you either. I wish I did, but everything is just kind of blah. Our life together isn't really together at all. We just live our lives separately while living in the same house, passing each other every now and then, inquiring about calendars and common events. We even manage to smile, but it's all lies. There's no feeling behind it."

"The point, here, Tom," I heard Bud say, calling me back from my troubles, "is that we can sense how others are feeling toward us. Given a little time, we can always tell when we're being coped with, manipulated, or outsmarted. We can always detect the hypocrisy. We can always feel the blame concealed beneath veneers of niceness. And we typically resent it. It won't matter if the other person tries managing by walking around, sitting on the edge of the chair to practice active listening, inquiring about family members in order to show interest, or using any other skill learned in order to be more effective. What we'll know and respond to is how that person is *regarding* us when doing those things."

My thoughts turned to Chuck Staehli again. "Yeah, I know what you're talking about," I said. "Do you know Chuck Staehli, the COO over at Tetrix?"

"About six feet, four inches, thinning reddish hair, narrow intense eyes?" asked Bud.

"That's him. Well, it took me about 10 minutes with him to know that he felt the world revolved around him—and if the world, then certainly everyone in his organization. I remember, for example, being on a conference call with Joe Alvarez after a hectic October spent fixing a bug in one of our products. It was a Herculean effort that consumed nearly all of my time and 80 percent of the time of one of my groups.

On the call, Joe offered congratulations for a job well done. Guess who accepted all the praise?"

"Staehli?"

"Yes, Staehli. He didn't even acknowledge us—or if he did, it was in such an undervalued way that it was worse than if he hadn't. He just lapped it all up and basked in the glory. I think in that moment he really thought he *was* responsible. It made me sick, quite frankly. And that's just one of many examples."

Bud was listening with interest, and suddenly I became aware of what I was doing—lampooning my old boss in front of my new one. I felt that I should shut up. Immediately. "Anyway, it just seemed that Chuck was a good example of what you're talking about." I sat back in my chair to signal that I was done, hoping that I hadn't said too much.

If Bud was alarmed by anything, he didn't show it.

"Yeah, that's a good example," he said. "Now compare Staehli to Lou. Or more precisely, compare the *influence* that each of them had on others. Would you say, for example, that Staehli inspired in you the same kind of effort, the same level of results, as Lou inspired in me?"

That was easy. "No way," I said. "Staehli didn't inspire hard work or devotion at all. Don't get me wrong. I worked hard anyway because I had a career of my own to worry about. But no one ever went out of his or her way to help him."

"Notice that some people—like Lou, for example— inspire devotion and commitment in others, even when they're interpersonally clumsy," said Bud. "The fact that they haven't attended many seminars or that they've never learned the latest techniques hardly matters. They produce! And they inspire those around them to do the same. Some of the best leaders in our company fall in this category. They don't always say or do the 'right' things, but people love working with them. They get results.

"But then there are other people—like Chuck Staehli, as you described him—who have a very different influence. Even if they do all the 'right' things interpersonally—even if they apply all the latest skills and techniques to their communications and tasks—it won't matter. People ultimately resent them and their tactics. And so they end up failures as leaders—failures because they provoke people to resist them."

"That's true," I said. "Staehli was a smooth operator, but I held that against him because it always felt that I was being *'smoothed.'*

"But are you saying that people skills don't matter?" I added. "I'm not sure *that's* right."

"No. I'm certainly not saying that. What I'm suggesting is that people skills are never *primary*. In my experience, they can be valuable when used by people like Lou—they can reduce misunderstandings and clumsiness. But they're not so helpful when used by people like Staehli, as you described him, for they just create resentment in the people one is trying to 'skill'—or 'smooth,' as you say. Whether people skills are effective or not depends on something deeper."

"Something deeper?"

"Yes, deeper than behavior and skill. That's what Lou—and my reaction to him—taught me the day of that second meeting here at Zagrum. *And* what he taught me at the beginning of the very next day when he and I met for a day-long meeting."

"You mean—?"

"Yes, Tom," Bud answered, before I had voiced the question. "Lou did for me what I'm now beginning to do for you.

They used to be called 'Lou Meetings,'" he added with a grin and a knowing look in my direction.

"Remember, I have the same problem that you have."

6   *The Deep Choice That Determines Influence*

"So what's this something deeper?" I asked curiously.

"What I've already introduced to you—self-deception. Whether I'm *in* or *out of* the box."

"Okay," I said slowly, wanting to know more.

"As we've been talking about, no matter what we're doing on the outside, people respond primarily to how we're feeling about them on the inside. And how we're feeling about them depends on whether we're in or out of the box concerning them. Let me illustrate by giving you a couple of examples.

"About a year ago, I flew from Dallas to Phoenix on a flight that had open seating. I'd arrived early enough to have a rather early boarding number. While boarding, I overheard the boarding agent say that the plane was not sold out but that there would be very few unused seats. I felt lucky and relieved to find a window seat open with a vacant seat beside it about a third of the way back on the plane. Passengers still in need of seats continued streaming down the aisle, their eyes scanning and evaluating the desirability of their dwindling seating options. I set my briefcase on the vacant middle seat, took out that day's paper, and started to read. I remember peering over the top corner of the paper at the people who were coming down the aisle. At the sight of body language that said my briefcase's seat was being considered, I spread the paper wider, making the seat look as undesirable as possible. Do you get the picture?"

"Yeah."

"Good. Now let me ask you a question: On the surface, what *behaviors* was I engaged in on the plane—what were some of the things I was *doing?*"

"Well, you were being kind of a jerk, for one thing," I answered.

"Now that's certainly true," he said, breaking into a broad smile, "but it's not quite what I mean—not yet anyway. I mean, what specific actions was I taking on the plane? What were the things I was *doing*? What was my outward behavior?"

"Well, let's see," I said, thinking of the picture in my mind. "You were . . . taking two seats. Is that the kind of thing you mean?"

"Sure. What else?"

"Uh . . . you were reading the paper. You were watching for people who might want to sit in the seat next to you. To be very basic, you were sitting."

"Okay, good enough," said Bud. "Here's another question: While I was doing these behaviors, how was I seeing the people who were looking for seats? What were they to me?"

"I'd say that you saw them as threats, maybe nuisances or problems—something like that."

"Okay, good. Would you say that I considered the needs of those still looking for seats to be as legitimate as my own?"

"Not at all. Your needs counted, and everyone else's were secondary—if that," I answered, surprised by my bluntness. "You were kind of seeing yourself as the kingpin."

Bud laughed, obviously enjoying the comment. "Well said, well said."

When he stopped chuckling, he continued, more seriously. "You're right. On that plane, if others counted at all, their needs and desires counted far less than mine."

"Now compare that experience to this one: About six months ago, Nancy and I took a trip to Florida. Somehow there was a mistake in the ticketing process, and we weren't seated together. The flight was mostly full, and the flight

32

attendant was having a difficult time trying to find a way to seat us together. As we stood in the aisle of the plane, trying to figure out a solution, a woman holding a hastily folded newspaper came up from behind us, from the rear of the plane, and said, 'Excuse me, if you need two seats together, I believe the seat next to me is vacant, and I'd be happy to sit in one of your seats.'

"Now think of this woman. How would you say that she saw us—did she see *us* as threats, nuisances, or problems?"

"No, not at all. It seems like she just saw you as people in need of seats who would like to sit together," I said. "That's probably more basic than what you're looking for, but—"

"No, that's great," said Bud, apparently about to make a point. "Compare this woman to me. Did she privilege her own needs and desires as I did mine?"

"It doesn't seem like she did," I answered. "It's sort of like from her point of view, under the circumstances, your needs and her needs counted about the same."

"That's right," Bud said as he walked away from me to his right toward the far end of the conference table. "Here we have two situations in which a person was seated on a plane next to an empty seat, evidently reading the paper and observing others who were still in need of seats on the plane. That's what was happening on the surface—behaviorally."

Bud opened two large mahogany doors at the far end of the table to my left, revealing a large whiteboard. "But notice how different this like experience was for me and for this woman. I minimized others; she didn't. I felt anxious, uptight, irritated, threatened, and angry, while she appears to have had no such negative emotions at all. I sat there blaming others who might be interested in my briefcase's seat—maybe one looked too happy, another too grim, another had too many carry-ons, another looked too talkative, and so on. She, on the other hand, appears not to have blamed but to have understood—whether happy, grim, loaded with carry-ons, talkative, or not—they needed to sit *somewhere*. And if so, why shouldn't the seat next to her—and in her case, even her *own* seat—be as rightly theirs as any others? Where I saw threats, nuisances, and problems, this woman simply saw people who would like to sit together.

"Now here's a question for you," Bud continued. "Isn't it the case that the people getting on both planes were people with comparable hopes, needs, cares, and fears and that all of them had more or less the same need to sit?"

That seemed about right. "Yes. I'd agree with that."

"If that's true, then I had a big problem—because I wasn't seeing the people on the plane like that at all. My view was that I somehow was entitled or superior to those who were still looking for seats. I was the 'kingpin,' as you say, and the people still looking for seats were somehow inferior and less deserving than me. Notice how my view of both myself and them was distorted from what we agreed was the reality—that is, that all of us were people with more or less the same need to sit. So my view of the world was a systematically incorrect way of seeing others and myself. I saw others as somehow less than they were—as objects with needs and desires somehow secondary and less legitimate than mine. But I couldn't see the problem with what I was doing. I was self-deceived—or, if you prefer, in the box.

"The lady who offered us her seat, on the other hand, saw others and the situation clearly, without bias. She saw others as they were, as people like herself, with similar needs and desires. She saw straightforwardly. She was out of the box.

"So the inner experiences of two people," he went on, "although they exhibited the same outward behaviors, were entirely different. And this difference is very important. I want to emphasize it with a diagram."

At this, he turned to the board and spent a minute drawing the following:

Behaviors
- Sitting next to empty seat
- Observing other passengers
- Reading the paper

Out of the Box
I see myself and others more or less as we are—as People

In the Box
I see myself and others in a systematically distorted way—others are mere Objects

"It's like this, Tom," Bud said, stepping to the side of the board so I could see. "Whatever I might be 'doing' on the surface—whether it be, for example, sitting, observing others, reading the paper, whatever—I'm being one of two fundamental ways when I'm doing it. Either I'm seeing others straightforwardly as they are—as people like me who have needs and desires as legitimate as my own—or I'm not. As I heard Kate put it once, one way, I experience myself as *a* person among people. The other way, I experience myself as *the*

35

person among objects. One way, I'm out of the box; the other way, I'm in the box. Does that make sense?"

I was thinking about a situation that had occurred a week earlier. Someone in my department had made herself into a terrible nuisance, and I couldn't see how this in-the-box and out-of-the-box distinction applied. In fact, if anything, the situation seemed to undercut what Bud was talking about. "I'm not sure," I said. "Let me give you a situation and you tell me how it fits."

"Fair enough," he said, taking his seat.

"I have a conference room around the corner from my office where I often go to think and strategize. The people in my department know that the room is kind of like a second office to me and are careful now, after a few altercations over the last month, not to schedule it without my knowing. Last week, however, someone in the department went in and used it. And not only that, she erased all my notes from the whiteboard. Can you believe that?"

"No, that's pretty bad," Bud said. "She never should have done that."

"That's what I thought too. I was furious. It took me a while to reconstruct what I had done, and I'm still not sure that I have everything right." I was about to tell more—about how I immediately had her called into my office, refused a handshake, and then told her without even asking her to sit down that she was never to do that again or she would be looking for a new job. But then I thought better of it. "How does self-deception fit into *that* scenario?" I asked.

"Well," Bud answered, "let me ask you a few questions, and then maybe you can tell me. Tell me what kinds of thoughts and feelings you had about this woman when you found out what she'd done."

"Well . . . I guess I thought she wasn't very careful—in fact, she was careless." Bud nodded with an inquisitive look that invited me to say more. "And I suppose I thought she was stupid to do what she did without asking somebody. And I thought she was pretty presumptuous and overly comfortable."

"It sounds that way to me too," Bud said. "Anything more?"

"No, that's about what I remember."

"Well let me ask you this: Do you know what she wanted to use the room for?"

"Well, no. But why should that matter? It doesn't change the fact that she shouldn't have been using it, does it?"

"Probably not," Bud answered. "But let me ask you another question: Do you know her name?"

The question caught me by surprise. I thought for a moment, but nothing came to me. I wasn't sure I'd ever heard her name. Had my secretary mentioned it? Or did she say it herself when she extended her hand to greet me? My mind searched for a memory, but there was nothing.

But why should that matter anyway, I thought to myself, emboldened. *So I don't know her name. So what? Does that make me wrong or something?* "No, I guess I don't know it, or I can't remember," I said.

Bud nodded his head, his hand on his chin. "Now here's the question I'd really like you to consider. Assuming that this woman is, in fact, careless, stupid, and presumptuous, do you suppose that she's *as* careless, stupid, and presumptuous as you accused her of being when all this happened?"

"Well, I didn't really accuse her."

"Not in your words, perhaps, but have you had any interaction with her since the incident?"

I thought of the ice-cold reception I gave her and the offer of her hand rebuffed. "Yeah, just once," I said more meekly.

Bud must have noticed the change in my voice, for he matched the change himself—dropping his voice slightly and losing his matter-of-fact tone. "Tom, I want you to imagine that you were her when you met. What do you think she felt from you?"

The answer, of course, was obvious. She couldn't have felt worse if I'd hit her with a two-by-four. Whereas before I'd barely considered her, I now remembered the tremor in her voice and her uncertain yet hurried steps as she left my office. I wondered now for the first time how I must have hurt her and what she must be feeling. I imagined that she must now be quite insecure and worried, especially since everyone in the department seemed to know about what had happened. "Yeah," I said slowly, "looking back on it, I'm afraid I didn't handle the situation very well."

"Then let me come back to my prior question," Bud continued. "Do you suppose that your view of this woman at the time made her seem systematically worse than she really was?"

I paused before answering, not because I wasn't sure, but because I wanted to collect my composure. "Well, maybe. I suppose it did. But that doesn't change the fact that she did something she shouldn't have, does it?" I added.

"Not at all. And we'll get to that. But right now, the question I want you to consider is this: Whatever she was doing— be it right or wrong—was your view of her more like *my* view of the people on the plane or more like the view of the woman I told you about?"

I sat there thinking about that for a moment.

"Think of it this way," Bud added, pointing at the diagram on the board. "Were you regarding her as a person like yourself, with similar hopes and needs, or was she just an object to you—as you said, just a threat, a nuisance, or a problem?"

"I guess she might've been just an object to me," I said finally.

"So now, how would you say this self-deception stuff applies? Would you say you were *in* or *out of* the box?"

"I guess I was probably *in* it," I said.

"That's worth thinking about, Tom. Because this distinction," he said, pointing again at the diagram, "reveals what was beneath Lou's success—and Zagrum's for that matter. Because Lou was usually out of the box, he saw straightforwardly. He saw people as they were—as people. And he found a way to build a company of people who see that way much more than people in most organizations do. If you want to know the secret of Zagrum's success, it's that we've developed a culture where people are simply invited to see others as people. And being seen and treated straightforwardly, people respond accordingly. That's what I felt—and returned—to Lou."

That sounded great, but it seemed too simplistic to be the element that set Zagrum apart. "It can't really be that simple, can it Bud? I mean, if Zagrum's secret were that basic, everyone would have duplicated it by now."

"Don't misunderstand," said Bud. "I'm not minimizing the importance of, for example, getting smart and skilled people into the company or working long and hard hours or any other number of things that are important to Zagrum's success. But notice—everyone else has duplicated all of *that* stuff, but they've yet to duplicate our results. And that's because they don't know how much smarter smart people are, how much more skilled skilled people get, and how much harder hardworking people work when they see, and are seen, straightforwardly—as people.

"And don't forget," he continued, "self-deception is a particularly difficult sort of problem. To the extent organizations are beset with self-deception—and most of them are—they can't see the problem. Most organizations are stuck in the box."

That claim hung in the air as Bud reached for his glass of water and took a drink.

"By the way," Bud added, "the woman's name is Joyce Mulman."

"Who . . . what woman?"

"The person whose hand you refused. Her name is Joyce Mulman."

7   *People or Objects*

"How do you know her?" I asked worriedly, my face failing to disconnect from my emotions. "And how'd you hear about what happened?"

Bud smiled reassuringly. "Don't be fooled by the distance between buildings. Word travels fast. I heard about it from a couple of your quality team leaders who were discussing it over lunch in the Building 5 cafeteria. It seems you made quite an impression."

I was regaining some composure and had managed to slacken the alarm from my face.

"As for knowing her," he continued, "I don't really, except that I try to know the names of as many people as I can around the company. It gets more difficult by the month with all of our growth, though."

I nodded in amazed agreement, shocked that someone in Bud's position would worry about knowing the name of someone who was at Joyce's level in the company.

"You know those pictures we take for clearance badges?"

I nodded.

"Well, the executive team members receive copies of all those pictures, and we try to familiarize ourselves with, if not completely memorize, the faces and names of the people who join the company.

"I have found, at least with me," Bud continued, "that if I'm not interested in knowing a person's name, I'm probably not really interested in the person as a person. For me, it's a basic litmus test. Now it doesn't necessarily work the other way—that is, I can learn and know people's names and have

41

them still be just objects to me. But if I'm unwilling even to try to remember someone's name, that itself is a clue to me that he or she is probably just an object to me and that I'm in the box. Anyway, that's why I know her—or at least how I know *of* her."

As Bud talked, my mind was taking inventory of the people in my division. I realized that of the 300 or so people in my organization, I knew only about 30 by name. *But I've been here only a month!* I said to myself in protest. *What more could you expect?* But I knew better. I knew that what Bud said about himself was true of me as well. The amount of time I had worked at Zagrum was a red herring. The truth was, I hadn't really *tried* to learn anyone's name. And as I thought about that now, it seemed clear that my lack of interest in as basic an issue as others' names was a pretty clear indication that I probably wasn't seeing them as people.

"I guess you think I really messed up," I said, my thoughts turning back to Joyce.

"It's not important what I think. What's important is what *you* think."

"Well, I'm kind of torn. On the one hand, I feel I owe Joyce an apology. But on the other hand, I still think she shouldn't have gone in that room and erased everything without checking first."

Bud nodded. "Do you suppose it's possible that you're right on both counts?"

"What? That I was wrong and right at the same time? How can that be?"

"Well, think of it this way," offered Bud. "You're saying that Joyce shouldn't just haul off and erase things that other people have written without finding out if that's okay first. Is that right?"

"Yes."

"And that seems perfectly reasonable to me as well. And you're saying that the right thing in the situation was to tell her that she must never do that again. Is that right?"

"Yes, that's the way it seems to me."

"Me too," said Bud.

"Then what did I do wrong?" I asked. "That's exactly what I did."

"Yes, that *is* what you did," Bud agreed, "but here's the question: Were you in the box or out of the box when you did it?"

All of a sudden a light went on for me. "Oh, I get it. It's not that I did the wrong thing necessarily but that I did what I did—maybe even the 'right' thing—in the wrong way. I was seeing her as an object. I was in the box. That's what you're saying."

"Exactly. And if you do what might on the surface be considered the right thing, but do it while in the box, you'll invite an entirely different and less-productive response than you would if you were out of the box. For remember, people respond not primarily to what you do but to how you're *being*—whether you're in or out of the box toward them."

This seemed to make sense, but I wasn't sure it was realistic for the workplace.

"Is there something you're wondering about?" Bud asked.

"Not really," I said without conviction, "Well, I *am* struggling with one thing."

"Sure, go ahead."

"I'm just sitting here wondering how you can conduct a business seeing others as people all the time. I mean, won't you get run over doing that? I can see it applying to family life, for example, but isn't it a bit unrealistic to think that you have to be that way at work too, when you've got to be fast and decisive?"

"I'm glad you asked that. It was the next thing I wanted to talk about.

"First," Bud continued, "I want you to think of Joyce. The way you handled the situation, I'd imagine that she won't ever be using your conference room again."

"Probably not."

"And since that's what you wanted to convey to her, you might think that your meeting with her was a success."

"Yeah, in a way I guess that's right," I said, feeling a bit better about what I'd done.

"Fair enough," Bud continued. "But let's think beyond the conference room. Do you think by being in the box when you conveyed your message that you invited in her *more* enthusiasm and creativity about her work or *less?*"

Bud's question caught me up short. All of a sudden, I realized that to Joyce Mulman, I was like Chuck Staehli. I remember being dressed down by Staehli, who seemed always in the box as near as I could tell, and I knew firsthand how demotivating it was as a result to work with him. To Joyce, I must seem no different from Staehli. The thought was terribly depressing. "I guess that's right. I might've solved the conference room problem but created other problems in its wake," I answered.

"It's worth thinking about," Bud agreed, nodding. "But your question actually goes to something deeper than that. Let me try to address it."

Bud stood up again and resumed his pacing, first to his right and then to his left. He seemed about to ask me a question, but then he paused, his hand to his face, apparently thinking. Then he said, "Explain to me what you understand now about being . . . " but he stopped that thought midsentence and paused again. "Sorry for the indecision here, Tom," he said. "Your question is such an important one, I want to make sure to handle it as helpfully as I can.

"Let's try it this way: Your question assumes that when we're out of the box, our behaviors are 'soft,' and when we're in the box, our behaviors are 'hard.' That's why you wonder, I take it, whether you can actually sustain a business being out of the box all the time. But let's think about that assumption a little harder. Is the distinction between being *in* the box and being *out of* the box a behavioral one?"

I thought about that for a minute. I wasn't certain, but it seemed like it might make a difference in behavior. "I'm not sure," I said.

"Well, let's look at the diagram," Bud said, pointing to what he had drawn on the board earlier. "Remember, this woman and I exhibited the same outward behaviors, but our experiences were completely different—I was *in* the box and she was *out*."

"Okay," I nodded.

"Here's an obvious question, but its implications are important," he continued. "Where on this diagram are behaviors listed?"

"Well, at the top," I said.

"And where are the in-the-box and out-of-the-box ways of being listed?"

"Beneath that, at the bottom."

"Yes," Bud said, turning away from the board and toward me. "What's the implication of this?"

I didn't know what he was after and sat silently, groping for an answer.

"What I mean," Bud added, "is that this diagram suggests that there are two ways to do . . . what?"

I studied the diagram, and then I saw it. "Oh yeah, there are two ways to do the behavior."

"So here's the question again: Is the distinction we're talking about fundamentally a distinction in behavior, or is it deeper than that?"

"It's deeper," I said.

"Now, let's think of Lou again for a minute. How would you characterize his behavior toward me? Remember, in a public forum, in front of my colleagues, he took from me a responsibility I had failed to accomplish, even though I'd accomplished everything else he'd asked me to do. And then he asked me if I would ever let him down again. How would you characterize his behavior toward me—would you say it was soft or hard?"

"That would definitely be hard," I said, "*too* hard even."

"Yes. But was he in the box or out of the box when he did it?"

"Out of the box."

"And how about you? How would you characterize your behavior toward Joyce—was it soft or hard?"

"Again, hard—perhaps too hard," I said, squirming slightly in my seat.

"You see," Bud said, as he walked back toward his chair across from me, "there are two ways to be hard. I can engage in hard behaviors and be either *in* the box or *out of* the box when I do them. The distinction isn't the behavior. It's the way I'm being when I am doing *whatever* I'm doing—be it soft *or* hard.

"Here's another way to think of it," he said. "If I'm out of the box, I'm seeing others as people. Fair enough?"

I nodded. "Yeah."

"Here's the question, then: Is the thing that a person needs always soft?"

"No, I guess it isn't. Sometimes people need a little hard encouragement," I said with a wry smile.

"That's right. And your situation with Joyce is a perfect example. She needed to be told that it was wrong to erase other peoples' notes from the board, and passing on that kind of message could be thought of as behaviorally hard. The point is that it's possible to deliver just that kind of hard message and still be out of the box when doing it. But it can be done out of the box only if the person you are delivering the message to is a *person* to you. That's what it *means* to be out of the box. And notice—and here's why this is so important— whose hard message likely invited a more productive response, Lou's or yours?"

I thought again of how demotivating it was to work for Chuck Staehli and about how I probably had the same kind of influence on Joyce as Chuck had on me. "Lou's," I answered. "Definitely."

"That's the way it seems to me too," Bud said. "So regarding hard behavior, here's the choice: We can be hard and invite productivity and commitment, or we can be hard and invite resistance and ill will. The choice isn't to be hard or not, it's to be in the box or not."

Bud looked at his watch. "It's now 11:30, Tom. I have a proposal. If it's okay with you, I'd like to break for an hour and a half or so."

I was surprised by the time. It didn't seem like we'd been at this for two and a half hours, but I was grateful for the break all the same. "Sure," I said. "So we'll get going again at 1:00, here?"

"Yes, that would be great. Now remember what we've covered so far: There's something deeper than behavior that determines our influence on others—it's whether we're in or out of the box. You don't know much about the box yet, but when we're in the box, our view of reality is distorted—we see neither ourselves nor others clearly. We are self-deceived. And that creates all kinds of trouble for the people around us.

"With that in mind," he continued, "I'd like you to do something for me before 1:00. I'd like you to think about the people here at Zagrum—both in and out of your department—and ask yourself whether you're in or out of the box toward them. And don't treat the people you're thinking about as one mass of people. Think of the individuals. You may be in the box toward one person and out of the box toward another at the same time. Think of the people."

"Okay, I will. Thanks, Bud; this has been very interesting. You've given me a lot to think about," I said as I started to stand up.

"Not nearly as much as you'll have to think about by this afternoon," Bud said with a chuckle.

8   *Doubt*

The August sun was sweltering overhead as I made my way back to the path that paralleled Kate's Creek. Although I grew up in St. Louis and had lived for years on the East Coast, I had spent enough time in milder climates to become permanently uncomfortable with the humidity that accompanied Connecticut's summer heat. I was grateful to slip beneath the trees as I turned in the direction of Building 8.

For the exposure I was feeling on the inside, however, there was no cover. I was on completely unfamiliar ground. Nothing I had experienced in my career had prepared me for my meeting with Bud. But although I was feeling quite unsure of myself and was far less convinced that I was on the top of the Zagrum advancement heap than I had been just a few hours before, I also had never felt better about what I was doing. I knew there was something I had to do during this break—I just hoped that Joyce Mulman was around to allow me to do it.

"Sheryl, could you tell me where Joyce Mulman's desk is?" I asked my secretary as I walked past her and into my office. As I turned from putting my notebook on the table, I noticed that Sheryl was standing at my door, a worried look on her face.

"What's wrong?" she asked slowly. "Has Joyce done something again?"

Sheryl's words implied concern for me, but her manner betrayed her concern for Joyce, as if she wanted to warn Joyce of an impending storm if she had the chance. And I was surprised by the assumption, implicit in her question, that if I wanted to see someone it must be because that person had done something wrong. My meeting with Joyce could wait for a minute. I needed to meet with Sheryl.

"No, nothing's wrong," I said. "Come in for a minute, though, there's something I want to talk to you about."

"Please, take a seat," I said, seeing her uncertainty. I walked around the desk and sat across from her.

"I'm new here," I began, "and you haven't had a lot of experience with me yet, but I want to ask you a question—and I need you to be absolutely candid with me."

"Okay," she said, noncommittally.

"Do you like working with me? I mean, compared to others you've worked for, would you say I'm a good boss?"

Sheryl squirmed in her seat, obviously uncomfortable with the question. "Sure," she offered in an overly eager voice. "Of course I like working for you. Why?"

"I'm just wondering," I said. "So you like working for me?"

She nodded unconvincingly.

"But would you say you like working with me as much as others you've worked for?"

"Oh, sure," she said with a forced smile, looking down at my desk. "I've liked everyone I've worked for."

My question put Sheryl in an impossible situation. It was supremely unfair. But I had my answer: She didn't like me much. The truth showed in her forced nonchalance and fidgeting discomfort. But I felt no ill will toward her. For the first time in a month, I felt sorry. I also felt a little embarrassed.

"Well, thank you, Sheryl," I said. "But I'm starting to feel that I've probably been kind of lousy to work with."

She didn't say anything.

I looked up and thought I noticed water forming in her eyes. Four weeks with her and I'd driven her to tears! I felt like the biggest heel. "I'm really sorry, Sheryl. Really sorry. I think I have some things to unlearn. I think I've been blind to some of the things I do to people. I don't know a lot about it yet, but I'm learning—how I sort of minimize others and don't see them as people. You know what I'm talking about?"

To my surprise, she nodded knowingly.

"You do?"

"Sure. The box, self-deception, and all of that? Yes. Everyone here knows about it."

"Did Bud talk to you too?"

"No, not Bud. He meets personally with all the new senior managers. There's a class here that everyone goes through where we learn the same things."

"So you know about the box—seeing others as people or seeing them as objects?"

"Yes, and self-betrayal, collusion, getting out of the box, focusing on results, the four levels of organizational performance, and all the rest."

"I don't think I've learned any of that stuff yet. At least Bud hasn't mentioned them. What was that—self- . . . ?"

"Betrayal," Sheryl said, filling in the gap. "It's how we get in the box in the first place. But I don't want to spoil what's coming. It sounds like you've only just started."

Now I *really* felt like a heel. It was one thing to treat another person as an object if she was as clueless to all these ideas as I had been, but knowing about the box, Sheryl had probably been seeing right through me the whole time.

"Boy, I've probably seemed like the biggest jerk to you, haven't I?"

"Not the biggest," Sheryl said with a smile.

Her wisecrack eased my mood, and I laughed. It was probably the first laugh between us in the four weeks we'd worked together, and in the ease of the moment that seemed like a real shame. "Well, maybe by this afternoon I'll know what to do about it."

"Maybe you know more about it than you think you do," she said. "By the way, Joyce is on the second floor, next to the pillar marked '8-31.'"

When I passed by Joyce's cubicle, it was empty. *She's probably at lunch,* I thought. I was about to leave, but then thought better of it: *If I don't do this now, who knows if I'll ever do it?* I sat down on an extra chair in the cubicle and waited.

The cubicle was plastered with pictures of two little girls—I'd say about three and five years old. And there were crayon drawings of happy faces, sunrises, and rainbows. I might have been sitting in a day-care center except for the piles of charts and reports stacked all around the floor.

I wasn't sure what Joyce did in the organization—*my* organization—which seemed pretty pathetic to me at the moment, but from the look of all the stacks of reports, I gathered that she was a member of one of our product quality teams. I was looking at one of the reports when she rounded the corner and saw me.

"Oh, Mr. Callum," she said in utter shock, stopping in her tracks, her hands to her face. "I'm sorry. I'm so sorry for the mess. It's not usually like this, really." She'd clearly been knocked off balance. I was the last person she probably ever expected to see in her cubicle.

"Don't worry about it. It's nothing compared to my office anyway. And please, call me Tom."

I could see the confusion in her face. She apparently had no idea what to say, or do, next. She just stood there at the entrance of her cubicle, trembling.

"I, uh, came to apologize, Joyce, for how I blew up at you about the conference room and all. That was really unprofessional of me. I'm sorry."

"Oh, Mr. Callum, I . . . I deserved it, I really did. I should never have erased your things. I've felt so bad about it. I've hardly slept in a week."

"Well, I think there probably was a way I could've handled it that wouldn't have left you sleepless."

Joyce broke out in an "Oh-you-didn't-have-to-do-that" smile and looked at the floor, pawing it with her toe. She'd stopped trembling.

It was 12:30. I had twenty or so minutes before I needed to make my way back over to continue with Bud. I was feeling pretty good and decided to call Laura.

"Laura Callum," said the voice on the other end.

"Hi," I said.

"Tom, I only have a second. What do you need?"

"Nothing. I just wanted to say hi."

"Is everything okay?" she said.

"Yeah, fine."

"You're *sure*."

"Yes. Can't I just call you to say hi without being interrogated?"

"Well, it's not like you ever call. There must be *something* going on."

"No, there's not. Nothing. Really."

"Okay, if you say so."

"Jeez, Laura. Why do you make everything so hard? I was just calling to see how you are."

"Well, I'm fine. And thanks for your concern, as always," she said, her voice dripping with sarcasm.

Everything that Bud had said that morning suddenly seemed far too naïve and simplistic. The box, self-deception, people or objects—all of those ideas may apply in some situations but not this one. Or if they did, who cares?

"Great. That's just great. Hope you have a nice afternoon," I said, matching her sarcastic tone and then some. "And I hope you're as cheerful and understanding with everyone there as you are with me."

The phone clicked dead.

No wonder I'm in the box, I thought as I hung up the phone. *Who wouldn't be, married to someone like that?*

I walked back to the Central Building full of questions. *First of all, what if someone else is in the box? What then? Like with Laura, it doesn't matter what I do. I called just to talk with her. And I was out of the box too. But then, with one swift emotionless stroke, she cut me off at the knees—just like she always does. She's the one with the problem. It doesn't matter what I do. Even if I am in the box, so what? What could you expect?*

Okay, I had a couple of good experiences with Sheryl and Joyce. But what else are they going to do? I mean, I run the division. They have to fall in line. And so what if Sheryl started to cry? Why should that be my fault? She has to be tougher than that. Anyone that weak deserves to cry—or at the very least, I shouldn't feel guilty if she does.

My anger grew with each step. *This is a waste of time,* I thought. *It's all so Pollyannaish. In a perfect world, okay. But blast it, this is business!*

Just then, I heard someone call my name. I turned to my left toward the voice. To my surprise it was Kate Stenarude, cutting her way across to me on the lawn.

PART II

How We Get IN *the Box*

9 *Kate*

I had met Kate just once. She'd been the final of my eight interviewers. I liked her instantly, as I'd since found out was common to nearly everyone in the company. Her story was in some ways the story of Zagrum, and like Zagrum's story, Kate's was freely passed along to new employees. She had joined the company fresh out of college—Williams College, I believe—some twenty-five years earlier, with a degree in history. One of the first twenty employees at Zagrum, she started as an order fulfillment clerk. In those days, it seemed that Zagrum's future was in perpetual doubt. After five years, by then Zagrum's director of sales, Kate left the company for a better opportunity, only to have her mind changed by a last-ditch personal appeal by Lou. Since that time, and until Lou's retirement, Kate had been second in command at Zagrum—Lou's "right-hand man," as it were. At Lou's retirement, she was elevated to president and CEO.

"Hello, Tom," she said, extending her hand to me. "It's good to see you again. Is life treating you well?"

"Yeah, I can't complain," I said, trying to ignore for the moment both my surprise at meeting her and the disaster that was my home life. "How about you?"

"Never a dull moment, I'm afraid," she said with a chuckle.

"I can't believe you remember who I am," I said.

"What? Forget a fellow St. Louis Cardinals fan? Never. And besides, I'm coming to meet with you."

"With *me?*" I said incredulously, pointing to my chest.

"Yes. Bud didn't say anything?"

"No. Or at least I don't think so. And I think I would've remembered *that*."

"Well, maybe he wanted it to be a surprise. I guess I ruined it for him," she said with a grin, apparently none too sorry. "I'm not often able to take part in these sessions, but I try to when my schedule allows. It's the thing I like most of all."

"Meeting hours on end talking about people's problems?" I said, trying to make a joke.

"Is that what you think's going on?" she said, a slight smile on her lips.

"No, I was just kidding. It's been pretty interesting actually, although I have a few questions about it."

"Good. I'd expect you would. And you're with the right person. There's no one better than Bud to learn all this from."

"But I've got to say, I'm amazed that you and Bud are both going to spend your afternoon with me. I mean, isn't there any more important use of your time?"

Kate stopped suddenly. And just as suddenly, I wanted to rephrase my question.

She looked at me seriously. "This may sound funny, Tom, but there really isn't anything more important than this—at least not from our viewpoint. Nearly everything we do here at Zagrum—from our job formulations to our reporting processes to our measurement strategies—is built on what you're now learning."

What does this have to do with measurement? I wondered. I couldn't see the connection.

"But I wouldn't expect you to have a feel for the seriousness of it yet. You've only just started. But I think I know what you're saying," she continued, starting now to walk again, although more slowly than before. "It does seem a little like overkill to have both me *and* Bud tied up with you this afternoon. And the truth is, it *is* overkill. I don't need to be there. Bud is much better at explaining it all than I am anyway. It's just that I like this stuff so much, if I could—if I didn't have all the other responsibilities that normally tie me down—I'd be there every time. Who knows? One day I might yank the responsibility from Bud and take it for myself," she said, laughing at the thought. "Today is one of the rare times I can come, although I might have to slip out a little early."

We walked for a moment in silence.

"Well, tell me how it's been going so far," she said.

"My work?"

"Your work . . . yes, but I really mean your experience *today*. How's it been going?"

"Well, other than being told that I'm in the box, it's going great," I replied, smiling as much as I could.

Kate laughed. "Yeah, I know what you mean. But don't take it too hard. Bud's in the box too you know," she said, with a gentle smile and a slight touch to my elbow. "And so am I for that matter."

"But if everyone's in the box anyway," I said, "including successful people like you and Bud, then what's the point?"

"The point is that although we're still sometimes in the box, and probably always will be to some extent, our success has come because of the times and ways that we at the company have been *out* of the box. The point of all this isn't perfection. Far from it. It's simply that we get better—better in systematic and concrete ways that improve the company's bottom line. That kind of leadership mentality—at every level of the organization—is what sets us apart.

"Part of the reason I come to these sessions when I can," she continued, "is to be reminded of some things. The box can be a pretty tricky place. You'll understand a lot more about that by the end of the day."

"But there's something I'm confused about right now, Kate."

"Only one thing?" she said, smiling, as we were climbing the staircase to the third floor.

"Well, maybe more than one, but here's one for starters. If there really are two ways of being—the out-of-the-box way where I see people as people and the in-the-box way where I see people as objects—what makes you one way or the other in the first place?" I was thinking of Laura and how impossible she is. "I mean, I'm thinking of a situation where it's impossible to be out of the box toward someone. Really impossible."

It seemed like I should continue the thought, or the question, whichever it was, but I couldn't think of anything else to say, so I just stopped.

"I think maybe Bud should be in on that answer," she said. "Here we are."

10 *Questions*

"Hi Tom," Bud said warmly as we came through the doors. "Did you have a good lunch?"

"It was too eventful for lunch, actually."

"Really? I look forward to hearing about it."

"Hey, Kate."

"Hi, Bud," she said, walking over toward the minifridge of juices. "Sorry I ruined your surprise."

"I didn't intend it as a surprise, actually. I just wasn't sure whether you'd actually be able to make it, so I didn't want to get Tom worked up for nothing. I'm glad you could come.

"Well, let's all sit down and get to it," Bud continued. "We're a little behind."

I situated myself in the same chair I had sat in that morning, my back to the window, about midway along the conference table. But as I did so, Kate, who was sizing up the room, suggested that we move closer to the whiteboard. Who was I to argue?

Kate sat in the seat nearest the board on the other side of the table, and I took the seat across from her, my back still to the window. She motioned Bud to sit between us at the head of the table, his back to the board. "Come on, Bud. It's your meeting."

"I was kind of hoping you'd take it over. You do this better than I do," he said.

"Oh, no I don't. I'll jump in now and then, but it's your show. I'm here to cheer you on . . . and to relearn a few things."

Bud sat down as directed, and Kate and Bud both smiled, obviously enjoying the friendly banter.

"Well, Tom. Before we move into some new things, why don't you review for Kate what we've done so far."

"Okay," I said, quickly collecting my thoughts.

I then reviewed for Kate what Bud had taught me about self-deception: how at any given moment we're either in or out of the box toward others; how, citing Bud's airplane examples, we can apparently do almost any outward behavior either in or out of the box but that whether we're in or out makes a huge difference in the influence we have on others. "Bud's been suggesting," I continued, "that success in an organization is a function of whether we're in the box or not and that our influence as leaders depends on the same thing."

"And I can't tell you how much I believe that," said Kate.

"I think I can kind of see it too," I said, wanting to be agreeable. "But Bud also said that this issue of whether we're in the box or not is at the heart of most of the people problems we see in organizations. I must admit I'm not altogether sure about *that* yet. And on the way over here, you said that Zagrum's reporting and measurement systems grow out of all this, and I'm *really* in the dark about how that would be."

"Yeah, I bet you are," Bud said, looking pleased. "By the time we go home tonight, I think you'll be starting to have a feel for all of that. At least I hope so. But before we move forward, you mentioned something about a busy hour and a half since we last met. Anything that pertains to what we've talked about?"

"Yeah, I think so."

I went on to tell them about Sheryl and Joyce. Bud and Kate seemed delighted, and I have to admit I got a little caught up in the experiences again as I recounted them.

"That all went really well. But then . . . " Without thinking, I almost launched into my problems with Laura. I caught myself just in time. "Then I called someone," I said.

Bud and Kate waited expectantly.

"I don't want to get into it much—it's sort of irrelevant to what we're doing here—but this person's pretty deep in the box, and all I have to do is talk with him and I'm in it too. And that's what happened when I called. I was out of the box, I'd just had these two good experiences, and I just wanted to call and see how he was doing. But he wouldn't let me do it. He wouldn't let me be out of the box. He just slammed me right back in. Under the circumstances, I think I did about as good a job as I could have done."

I'd expected Bud or Kate to say something to this, but both remained silent, as if inviting me to continue. "It's no big deal, really," I continued, "it's just that it has me a little confused."

"About what?" asked Bud.

"About the whole box thing to begin with," I said. "I mean, if others keep putting us in the box, what can we do about it? I guess what I want to know is, how can you get out of the box when someone keeps putting you in it?"

At this, Bud stood up, rubbing his face with his hand. "Well, Tom," he said, "we're certainly going to get to how we get out of the box. But first we have to understand how we get in it. Let me tell you a story."

11   *Self-Betrayal*

"Now at first you're going to think this is a silly story. It's not even a workplace story. We'll apply it to the workplace when we get a little more under our belts. Anyway, it's just a simple little story—mundane even. But it illustrates well how we get in the box in the first place.

"One night a number of years ago, when David was just an infant, I was awakened by his wailing cries. He was probably four months old or so at the time. I remember glancing at the clock. It was around 1:00 A.M. In the flash of that moment I had an impression or a sense or a feeling—a thought of something I should do. It was this: 'Get up and tend to David so Nancy can sleep.'

"Now this sort of sense is very basic," he continued. "We're all people. I've grown up as a person, as you have and Kate has. And when we're out of the box and seeing others as people, we have a very basic sense about others—namely, that like me, they too have hopes, needs, cares, and fears. And on occasion, as a result of this sense, we have impressions of things to do for others—things we think might help them, things we can do for them, things we *want* to do for them. You know what I'm talking about?"

"Sure, that's clear enough," I said.

"This was such an occasion—I felt a desire to do something for Nancy. But you know what?" he asked rhetorically, "I didn't act on it. I just stayed there, listening to David wail."

I could relate. I'd waited out Todd and Laura plenty of times.

"You might say I 'betrayed' my sense of what I should do for Nancy," he continued. "Now that's sort of a strong way to say it. But I just mean that in acting contrary to my sense of what was appropriate, I betrayed my own sense of how I should be toward another person. So we call such an act 'self-betrayal.'"

At that, he turned to the board to write. "Do you mind if I erase this diagram?" he asked, pointing at the diagram of the two ways of doing behavior.

"No, that's fine," I said. "I've got it."

In its place, in the top left corner of the board, he wrote the following:

"Self-betrayal"

1. An act contrary to what I feel I should do
   for another is called an act of "self-
   betrayal."

"Self-betrayal is the most common thing in the world, Tom," Kate added, in an easy manner. "Let me give you a few more examples.

"Yesterday I was at Rockefeller Center in New York. I got into the elevator, and as the door started to close I saw someone scurry around the corner and race toward the door. In that instant, I had a sense that I should catch the door for him. But I didn't. I just let it close, my last view being that of his outstretched, lunging arm. Have you ever had that experience?"

I had to admit I had.

"Or how about these: Think of a time you felt you should help your child or your spouse, but then decided not to. Or a time you felt you should apologize to someone, but never got around to doing it. Or a time when you knew you had some information that would be helpful to a coworker, but you kept it to yourself. Or a time when you knew you needed to stay late to finish some work for someone but went home instead—without bothering to talk to anyone about it.

"I could go on and on, Tom. I've done all of these, as I bet you have too."

I had to admit it. "Yeah, I'm afraid so."

"They're all examples of self-betrayal—times when I had a sense of something I should do for others but didn't do it."

Kate paused, and Bud joined back in.

"Now think about it, Tom. This is hardly a monumental idea. It's about as simple as it comes. But its implications are astounding. And astoundingly unsimple. Let me explain.

"Let's go back to the baby crying story. Picture the moment. I felt I should get up so Nancy could sleep, but then I didn't do it. I just stayed lying there next to Nancy, who also was just lying there."

As Bud was saying this, he drew the following in the middle of the board:

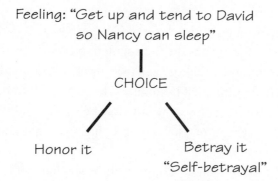

Feeling: "Get up and tend to David so Nancy can sleep"

CHOICE

Honor it   Betray it "Self-betrayal"

"Now—in this moment, as I'm just lying there listening to our wailing child, how do you imagine I might've started to see, and feel about, Nancy?"

"Well, she probably seemed kind of lazy to you," I said.

"Okay, 'lazy,'" Bud agreed, adding it to the diagram.

"Inconsiderate," I added. "Maybe unappreciative of all you do. Insensitive."

"These are coming pretty easy to you, Tom," Bud said with a wry smile, adding what I'd said to the diagram.

"Yeah, well, I must have a good imagination, I guess," I said, playing along. "I wouldn't know any of this for myself."

"No, of course you wouldn't," said Kate. "Nor would you either, would you, Bud? The two of you are probably too busy sleeping to be aware of any of this," she said, chuckling.

"Aha, the battle is joined," laughed Bud. "But thank you, Kate. You raise an interesting point about sleeping." Turning back to me, he asked, "What do you think, Tom? Was Nancy really asleep?"

"Oh . . . maybe, but I doubt it."

"So you think she was faking it—pretending to sleep?"

"That'd be my guess," I said.

Bud wrote "faker" on the diagram.

"But hold on a minute, Bud," Kate objected. "Maybe she *was* just asleep—and probably, from the sounds of it, because she's so worn out from doing everything for *you*," Kate added, obviously happy with the jab.

"Okay, good point," Bud said with a grin. "But remember, whether she actually was asleep is less important right now than whether I was *thinking* she was asleep. We're talking now about my perception once I betrayed myself. *That's* the point."

"I know," said Kate with a smile, settling back into her chair. "I'm just having fun, enjoying the protection of anonymity. If it were my example, you'd have plenty to pile on about."

"So from the perspective of that moment," Bud continued again, looking at me, "if she was just feigning sleep and letting her child wail, what kind of mom do you suppose I thought she was being?"

"Probably a pretty lousy one," I said.

"And what kind of wife?"

"Again, pretty lousy—inconsiderate, thinks you don't do enough, and so on."

Bud wrote this on the diagram as well.

"So, here I am," he said, backing away from the diagram and reading what he had written. "Having betrayed myself, we can imagine that I might've started to see my wife in that moment as 'lazy,' 'inconsiderate,' 'taking me for granted,' 'insensitive,' a 'faker,' a 'lousy mom,' and a 'lousy wife.'"

"Wow, Bud. Congratulations," said Kate, sarcastically. "You've managed to completely vilify one of the best people I know."

"I know. It's scary, isn't it?"

"I'll say."

"But it's worse than that, even," Bud continued. "That's how I started to see *Nancy*. But having betrayed myself, how do you suppose I started to see *myself*?"

"Oh, you probably saw yourself as the victim," Kate said, "as the poor guy who couldn't get the sleep he needed."

"That's right," Bud said, adding "victim" to the diagram.

"And you would've seen yourself as hardworking," I added. "The work you had to do the next morning probably seemed pretty important to you."

"Good, Tom, that's right," Bud said, adding "hardworking" and "important."

"How about this?" he asked after a pause, "What if I'd gotten up the night before? How do you suppose I would've seen myself if that were the case?"

"Oh, as 'fair,'" Kate answered.

"Yes. And how about this?" he added. "Who is sensitive enough to hear the child?"

I had to laugh. All of this—the way Bud saw Nancy and the way he saw himself—seemed on the one hand so absurd and laughable but on the other hand so common. "Well *you* were the sensitive one, obviously," I said.

"And if I'm sensitive to my child, then what kind of dad do I think I am?"

"A *good* one," Kate answered.

"Yes. And if I'm seeing myself as all of these," he said, pointing to the board—"if I see myself as 'hardworking,' 'fair,' 'sensitive,' a 'good dad,' and so on—then what kind of husband do I think I am?"

"A *really* good husband—especially putting up with a wife like the one you were thinking you had," Kate said.

"Yes," Bud said, adding to the diagram. "So look what we have."

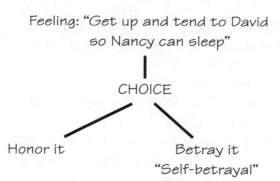

Feeling: "Get up and tend to David
so Nancy can sleep"

CHOICE

Honor it   Betray it
                      "Self-betrayal"

How I started to see myself	How I started to see Nancy
Victim	Lazy
Hardworking	Inconsiderate
Important	Unappreciative
Fair	Insensitive
Sensitive	Faker
Good dad	Lousy mom
Good husband	Lousy wife

"Now let's think about this diagram. For starters, look at how I started to see Nancy after I betrayed myself—as lazy, inconsiderate, and so on. Now think of this: Do any of these thoughts and feelings about Nancy invite me to reconsider my decision and do what I felt I should do for her?"

"No. Not at all," I said.

"What *do* they do for me?" Bud asked.

"Well, they justify your *not* doing it. They give you reasons to stay in bed and *not* tend to David."

"That's right," Bud said, turning to the board. He added a second sentence to his description of self-betrayal:

"Self-betrayal"

1. An act contrary to what I feel I should do for another is called an act of "self-betrayal."
2. When I betray myself, I begin to see the world in a way that justifies my self-betrayal.

"If I betray myself," Bud said as he backed away from the board, "my thoughts and feelings will begin to tell me that I'm justified in whatever I'm doing or failing to do."

Bud sat back down, and I started to think of Laura.

"For a few minutes," he said, "I want to examine *how* my thoughts and feelings do that."

12 *Characteristics of Self-Betrayal*

"To begin with, think about this: When did Nancy seem worse to me, before I betrayed myself or afterward?"

"Afterward, for sure," I said, his question pulling me back to his story.

"Yes," said Bud, "and when do you suppose sleep seemed more important to me, before I betrayed myself, or after?"

"Oh, I guess after."

"And when do you suppose other interests—like my work responsibilities the next morning, for example—seemed more pressing to me, before I betrayed myself or after?"

"Again, after."

Bud paused for a moment.

"Now here's another question: Take a look again at how I started to see Nancy. Do you suppose that she's in reality as bad as she seemed to me after I betrayed myself?"

"No, probably not," I said.

"I can vouch for Nancy," said Kate. "The woman described up there bears no resemblance."

"That's true," Bud agreed.

"Yeah, but what if she did?" I interjected. "I mean, what if she really *was* a lazy and inconsiderate person, and even a bad wife, for that matter? Wouldn't that make a difference?"

"That's a good question, Tom," Bud said, rising again from his chair. "Let's think about that for a minute."

He started to pace the length of the table. "Let's just say, for the sake of argument, that Nancy *is* lazy. And let's assume that she's generally inconsiderate too. Here's the question: If she's lazy and inconsiderate after I betrayed myself, then she must've been lazy and inconsiderate before, right?"

"Yes," I answered. "If she's lazy and inconsiderate, she's lazy and inconsiderate—before, after, it wouldn't matter."

"Okay, good," said Bud. "But if that's the case, then notice—I felt I should get up and help her *even though* she was lazy and inconsiderate. Before I betrayed myself, I didn't see her faults as reasons not to help her. I felt that way only *after* I betrayed myself, when I used her faults as justifications for my own misbehavior. Does that make sense?"

I wasn't sure. It seemed like it probably made sense, but the discussion made me uncomfortable because I had an example of this situation in my own house. Laura *was* inconsiderate, although perhaps not lazy. And it sure seemed to me that she was a pretty lousy wife. At least she had been recently. And it seemed like that was relevant to whether she deserved help from me or not. It's hard to want to help someone who shows no feelings for you. "I guess that makes sense," I said, still troubled and unsure how and whether to express my concerns.

"Here's another way to think of it," Bud said, sensing my uncertainty. "Remember what we were just talking about. Even if Nancy really is lazy and inconsiderate, when do you suppose she would've seemed *more* lazy and inconsiderate to me—before I betrayed myself or after?"

"Oh yeah," I said, remembering the earlier point. "After."

"That's right. So even if she *is* lazy and inconsiderate, the truth is that in self-betrayal, I'm making her out to be more lazy and inconsiderate than she really is. And that's something *I'm* doing, not something she's doing."

"Okay, I get that," I said, nodding.

"So think about it," Bud continued. "Here I am in self-betrayal, and I think that I'm not getting up to help Nancy because of what she's doing to me — because she's lazy, inconsiderate, and so on. But is that the truth?"

I looked at the diagram. "No," I said, beginning to see the picture. "You *think* that's the truth, but it's not."

"That's right. The truth is, her faults seemed relevant to whether I should help her only *after I failed to help her*. I focused on and inflated her faults when I needed to feel justified for *mine*. Having betrayed myself, the truth was just the opposite of what I thought it was."

"Yeah, I guess that's right," I said, nodding my head slowly. This was getting pretty interesting. But I was still wondering how Laura fit into it.

"That's how Bud's view of Nancy was distorted," Kate added, "but consider how his view even of himself became distorted. Do you suppose that he's really as hardworking, important, fair, and sensitive as he was claiming himself to be? He was experiencing himself as a good dad and husband, for example, but in that moment, was he in actual fact *being* a good dad and husband?"

"No. That's right, he wasn't," I said. "At the same time he was inflating Nancy's faults, he was also minimizing his own. He was inflating his own virtue."

"Yes," said Kate.

"So think about it," Bud said, jumping back into the conversation. "Was I seeing myself clearly after I betrayed myself?"

"No."

"How about Nancy? Was I seeing *her* clearly after I betrayed myself?"

"No. You weren't seeing anything very clearly," I said.

"So once I betrayed myself, my view of reality became distorted," Bud said in summary, turning toward the board. He added a third line to the description of self-betrayal:

"Self-betrayal"

1. An act contrary to what I feel I should do for another is called an act of "self-betrayal."
2. When I betray myself, I begin to see the world in a way that justifies my self-betrayal.
3. When I see a self-justifying world, my view of reality becomes distorted.

"So, Tom," Bud said, after we'd paused to read what he'd written, "where was I after I betrayed myself?"

"Where *were* you?" I asked, trying to figure out the question.

"Yeah, where was I?" Bud repeated, refusing to let me off the hook.

"Think about it," he continued. "Before I betrayed myself, I simply saw something I could do to help Nancy. She was a person with a need that I felt I should fill. I saw the situation straightforwardly. But after I betrayed myself, my view both of her and myself became distorted. I saw the world in a way that justified my failure. My perception became distorted systematically in my favor. When I betrayed myself, I became self-deceived."

"Oh, I see it," I said, enthusiastically. "So when you betrayed yourself, you entered the box. That's what you mean. That's the answer to your question of where you were—isn't it?"

"Exactly," he said, turning again and writing on the board. "Self-betrayal is how we enter the box."

"Self-betrayal"

1. An act contrary to what I feel I should do for another is called an act of "self-betrayal."
2. When I betray myself, I begin to see the world in a way that justifies my self-betrayal.
3. When I see a self-justifying world, my view of reality becomes distorted.
4. So—when I betray myself, I enter the box.

"Based on this discussion, I think we should add a few summary elements to your diagram, Bud," Kate said, standing and moving toward the board.

"Sure, go ahead," he said, taking his seat.

First she drew a box around the side of Bud's diagram that described his experience in self-betrayal. Then, to the side, she wrote, "When I betray myself, I enter the box—I become self-deceived."

"Now," she said, turning to me. "I want to pull together and summarize from Bud's story four key characteristics of self-betrayal. And as I do it, I'm going to list them right here on this diagram.

"First of all," she said, "remember how after Bud betrayed himself, he made Nancy worse than she was?"

"Yeah," I nodded. "He inflated her faults."

"Exactly."

Kate added "Inflate others' faults" to the diagram.

"And what about Bud's *own* faults?" she said. "Did he see them straightforwardly after he betrayed himself?"

"No," I answered. "He sort of ignored his own faults and just focused on Nancy's."

"That's right."

She added "Inflate own virtue" to the diagram.

"And do you remember what happened to the perceived importance of things such as sleep and fairness after Bud betrayed himself?" she asked.

"Yes. They seemed more important after he betrayed himself than they did before."

"That's right. After Bud betrayed himself, the perceived importance of anything in the situation that could provide justification for his self-betrayal became inflated—like, for example, the importance of sleep, fairness, and his responsibilities the next day."

She added "Inflate the value of things that justify my self-betrayal" to the diagram.

"Okay," Kate said. "One more. When in this story did Bud start to *blame* Nancy?"

I looked at the diagram. "When he betrayed himself," I answered.

"That's right. He wasn't blaming her when he just felt he should help her. Only after he failed to help her."

She added "Blame" to the diagram.

"And after I betrayed myself, consider how blame-filled my experience was," Bud added. "Those things on the diagram are all thoughts I had about Nancy, but consider what my *feelings* toward her became after I got in the box. For example, do you suppose I felt irritated?"

"Yes. Absolutely," I said.

"But notice," Bud said, drawing my attention to the diagram. "Did I feel irritated toward her when I just felt I should help?"

"No."

"And how about anger? Do you suppose I felt angry after I got in the box?"

"Oh yeah. Just look at the way you were seeing her. If my wife seemed that way, I'd be plenty mad at her." I was jolted by my own comment because as I looked at the diagram, my wife *did* seem that way to me.

"You're right," agreed Bud. "I think I was plenty upset at what I viewed to be her insensitivity to my situation. So notice, my blaming didn't stop with my thoughts. In the box, my *feelings* blamed too. They said, 'I'm irritated because you're irritating, and I'm angry because you've done things to *make* me angry.' In the box, my *whole way* was blaming—both my thoughts and my feelings told me Nancy was at fault.

"And just to be clear here," he continued, "*was* Nancy to blame? Was I irritated and angry because of Nancy, like my irritation and anger were telling me? Were my thoughts and feelings telling me the truth?"

I thought for a moment. I wasn't sure. It seemed strange that feelings could lie, if that's what Bud was suggesting.

"Think about it this way," Bud went on, pointing to the board. "What's the only thing that happened in this story between the time that I wasn't irritated and angry and the time I was?"

I looked at the diagram.

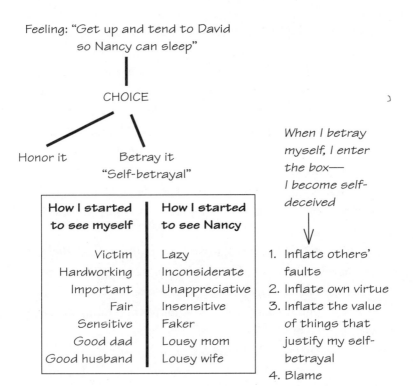

"Your choice not to do what you felt you should do," I said. "Your self-betrayal."

"That's right. That's all that happened. So what caused my irritation and anger at Nancy?"

"Your self-betrayal," I said, my voice trailing off as I became lost in the implications of this thought. *Really? Is that right?* I looked again at the diagram. Before he betrayed himself, Bud saw Nancy, whatever her faults, simply as a person who could use his help. I understood that. But after he betrayed himself, she seemed very different to him. She didn't seem to *deserve* help anymore, and Bud thought he felt that way because of how *she* was being. But that wasn't true.

The only thing that happened was his own self-betrayal. So Bud's feelings *were* lying to him!

But that can't be my *case!* I screamed in my mind. *Laura really is a problem. I'm not just imagining it—and heaven knows I'm not making it up. I mean, there's no tenderness or caring in her at all. She's like a cool steel blade. And I know the pain of that blade. She uses it with skill. And Bud's telling me that's* my *fault? What about Laura? Why isn't it* her *fault?*

That thought caught me. *That's right,* I told myself. *Maybe it* is *her fault. She's the one who's betraying herself.* I started to feel better.

But wait, I argued with myself. *I'm blaming. That thought itself is a blaming. And blaming is something that Bud started doing* after *he betrayed himself, not before.*

Yeah, but so what? I fired back at myself. *If Laura's the one wielding the blade, I'm justified in blaming.*

But why do I need to feel justified?

Oh, blast it! Why am I questioning myself? I thought. *Laura's the one with the problem.*

But that's what Bud thought too, I remembered.

I felt trapped between what I thought I knew and what I was learning. Either this stuff was all wet or I was. I was a mass of confusion.

Then I saw a way out.

13 Life in the Box

I looked up at the board again.

Yes! I cheered silently. *All of this trouble happened because Bud betrayed a feeling that he had for Nancy. But I rarely have those kinds of feelings for Laura. And the reason why is obvious—Laura is so much* worse *than Nancy. No one would feel they should do things for her given the way she is. My case is different. Bud got into trouble because he betrayed himself. I'm not betraying* myself. I sat back, satisfied.

"Okay, I think I get this," I said, preparing to ask my question. "I think I understand the idea of self-betrayal. Check me on it: As people, we have a sense of what other people might need and how we can help them. Right?"

"Yes," Bud and Kate said, almost in unison.

"And if I have that sort of a sense and go against it, then I betray my own sense of what I should do for someone. That's what we call self-betrayal. Right?"

"That's right. Yes."

"And if I betray myself, then I start seeing things differently—my view of others, myself, my circumstances, everything is distorted in a way that makes me feel okay about what I'm doing."

"Yes, that's right," Bud said. "You begin to see the world in a way that makes you feel justified in your self-betrayal."

"Okay," I said, "I understand that. And that's what you call 'the box.' I go into the box when I betray myself."

"Yes."

"Okay. Then here's my question: What if I don't have a feeling that I betray? For example, what if when a child cries

I don't have a feeling like the one you had? What if I just elbow my wife and tell her to get the kid? What you're saying is that it's not self-betrayal and that I wouldn't be in the box, right?"

Bud paused for a moment. "That's an important question, Tom. We need to think about it with some care. As for whether you'd be in the box or not, I wouldn't know. You'll have to think of situations in your life and decide for yourself. But there's something we haven't talked about yet that may help you with your question.

"So far we've learned how we get *in* the box. At this point we're ready to consider how we carry boxes with us."

"How we carry them with us?" I asked.

"Yes." Bud stood up and pointed at the diagram. "Notice that after I betrayed myself, I saw myself in certain self-justifying ways. For example, I saw myself as the sort of person who's 'hardworking,' 'important,' 'fair,' 'sensitive,' the sort of person who's a 'good dad' and a 'good husband.' That's how I saw myself after I betrayed myself. But here's an important question: Was I lying there thinking of myself in these self-justifying ways *before* I betrayed myself?"

I thought about the question. "No, I wouldn't think so."

"That's right. These self-justifying ways of seeing myself arose in my self-betrayal—*when I needed to be justified.*"

"Okay, that makes sense," I said.

"But think about it," Bud continued. "The story of self-betrayal we've been talking about is just one simple example, and it happened many years ago. Do you think it's the only time I've ever betrayed myself?"

"I doubt it," I said.

"You can do more than doubt it," Bud said, chuckling. "I don't think I've ever gone a day without betraying myself in some way—and perhaps not even an hour. I've spent a *life-time* betraying myself, as have you, Kate, and everyone else at Zagrum. And every time I've betrayed myself, I've seen myself in certain self-justifying ways—just like I did in the story we've been talking about. The result is that over time, certain of these self-justifying images become *characteristic* of me. They're the form my boxes take as I carry them with me into new situations."

At this, Bud added a fifth sentence to the list about self-betrayal:

"Self-betrayal"

1. An act contrary to what I feel I should do for another is called an act of "self-betrayal."
2. When I betray myself, I begin to see the world in a way that justifies my self-betrayal.
3. When I see a self-justifying world, my view of reality becomes distorted.
4. So—when I betray myself, I enter the box.
5. Over time, certain boxes become charac-teristic of me, and I carry them with me.

I sat there trying to digest the meaning of all this, but I wasn't quite sure I understood.

"Let me show you what I mean. Let's take this self-justifying image right here," Bud said, pointing on the diagram to "Good husband." "Let's imagine that over many self-betrayals, this self-justifying image has become characteristic of me. So as I move through my marriage and my life, I see myself as the sort of person who's a good husband. Fair enough?"

I nodded.

"Now consider this: It's Mother's Day, and near the end of the day my wife says in a hurt voice, 'I don't think you thought about me much today.'"

Bud paused, and I thought about Mother's Day at my own house a few months earlier. Laura had said almost the same thing.

"If I'm carrying a self-justifying image that says 'I'm the sort of person who's a good husband,' how do you suppose I might start to see Nancy when she accuses me of not thinking about her? Do you suppose I might start to feel defensive and blame her?"

"Oh, absolutely," I said, thinking of Laura. "You'd blame her for failing to notice or give you credit for all the things you *do* do, for example."

"Yes. So I might blame her for being ungrateful."

"Or for even more than that," I added. "You might feel trapped by her. I mean, there she is, accusing you of being uncaring, when she's the one who hardly ever cares for *you*. It's hard to throw yourself into making her day wonderful when she herself never does anything that would make you want to do that in the first place." I stopped myself short as I felt the cool wind of embarrassment against my soul. Bud's story had transported me to my own troubles, and my indiscretion had given Bud and Kate a peek at the raw emotion I felt toward Laura. I cursed myself and resolved to stay more detached.

"That's right," Bud said. "I know exactly what you mean. And when I'm feeling that way toward Nancy, do you suppose I might also inflate her faults? Might she seem worse to me than she really is?"

I didn't want to answer, but Bud waited. "Yeah, I suppose so," I said flatly.

"And notice something else," Bud continued enthusiastically. "As long as I'm feeling that way, will I ever seriously consider Nancy's complaint—that I hadn't really thought of her? Or will I be more likely to brush it off?"

I thought of an endless string of altercations with Laura. "You probably wouldn't question yourself much," I said finally, without much enthusiasm.

"Here I am," Bud continued, pointing to the board, "blaming Nancy, inflating her faults, and minimizing my own. So where am I?"

"I guess you're in the box," I answered, half-audibly, while my mind argued the point—*But what about Nancy? Maybe she's in the box too. Why don't we consider* that? I suddenly started to feel very angry with this—all of it.

"Yes," I heard Bud say, "but notice—did I have to have a feeling that I betrayed in that moment in order to be in the box toward her?"

The question didn't quite register. "What was that?" I asked belligerently.

The edge in my voice caught me by surprise, and I felt exposed once again. My resolution of detachment had held for all of a minute. "I'm sorry, Bud," I said, trying to recover, "I didn't quite catch the question."

Bud looked at me gently. It was clear that he'd noticed my anger, but he didn't seem put off by it. "Well, my question was this: Here I am in the box toward Nancy—I was blaming her, inflating her faults, and so on—but did I have to have a feeling that I betrayed in that moment in order to be in the box toward her?"

For some reason, this brief exchange and the focus required by Bud's question calmed me, or at least took my mind off my troubles for a moment. I thought about his story. I couldn't remember him mentioning a feeling that he betrayed. "I'm not sure," I answered. "I guess not."

"That's right. I didn't have to have a feeling that I betrayed in that moment in order to be in the box *because I was already in the box*."

I must have looked a bit puzzled because Kate jumped in with an explanation.

"Remember what Bud was just talking about, Tom. Over time, as we betray ourselves, we come to see ourselves in certain self-justifying ways. We end up carrying these self-justifying images with us into new situations, and to the extent we do, we enter new situations *already* in the box. We don't see people straightforwardly, as people. Rather, we see them *in terms of* the self-justifying images we've created. If people act in ways that challenge the claim made by a self-justifying image, we see them as threats. If they reinforce the claim made by a self-justifying image, we see them as allies. If they fail to matter to a self-justifying image, we see them as unimportant. Whichever way we see them, they're just objects to us. We're already in the box. That's Bud's point."

"Exactly," Bud agreed. "And if I'm already in the box toward someone, I generally won't have feelings to do things for them. So the fact that I have few feelings to help someone isn't necessarily evidence that I'm out of the box. It may rather be a sign that I'm deep within it."

"So you're saying that if I generally don't have feelings to do things for someone in my life—say, for my wife, Laura—I'm probably in the box toward that person? Is that what you're saying?" I asked.

"No, not exactly," answered Bud, as he took his seat next to mine. "I'm suggesting that that's the way it generally is for *me*—at least for those I'm closest to in my life. Whether it's the same with you, toward Laura, for example, I don't know. You'll have to wrestle with that for yourself. But as a general rule, let me suggest this: If you seem to be in the box in a given situation but can't identify a feeling that you betrayed in that moment, that's a clue that you might *already* be in the box. And you may find it useful to wonder whether you're carrying around some self-justifying images."

"Like being the sort of person who's a good spouse, for example?" I asked.

"Yes. Or the sort of person who's important or competent or hardworking or the smartest. Or being the sort of person who knows everything or does everything, or doesn't make mistakes or thinks of others, and so on. Almost anything can be perverted into a self-justifying image."

"Perverted? What do you mean?"

"I mean that most self-justifying images are the in-the-box perversions of what would be great out of the box. For example, it's great to be a good spouse. That's exactly what we should be for our spouses. And it's great to think of others and to try to be as knowledgeable as we can be in whatever areas we work in. And so on. But these are the very things we're *not* being when we have self-justifying images about them."

"I'm not sure I understand," I said.

"Well," Bud said, standing again, "let's think about self-justifying images for a minute." He resumed his pacing. "For example, certainly it's good to think of others, but who am I thinking of when I'm thinking of myself as the sort of person who thinks of others?"

"Yourself, I guess."

"Exactly. So my self-justifying image lies to me. It tells me I'm focused on one thing—in this case, others—but in having that image I'm actually focused on myself."

"Okay, fair enough," I said, looking for holes in his logic. "But what about the one you mentioned about being smart or knowing everything? What's the problem with that?"

"Let's think about it. Let's say you have a self-justifying image that says you know everything. How do you suppose you'd feel toward someone who suggested something new to you?"

"I guess I'd resent him. I might find something wrong with his suggestion."

"Right. So would he keep coming to you with new ideas?"

"Probably not."

"And would you end up learning new things?"

"No, I guess not. Oh, I see your point," I said suddenly. "My self-justifying image about being learned can be the very thing that sometimes *keeps* me from learning."

"Yes. So if I have that self-justifying image, is knowing everything really what I'm most concerned about?"

"Not really. I guess your major concern is yourself—how you look."

"Exactly," Bud said. "That's the nature of most self-justifying images."

Bud continued, but I was no longer paying attention. I became lost in my own thoughts. *Okay, so I can carry my boxes with me. Maybe I have some of these self-justifying images that Bud is talking about. Maybe I'm in the box toward Laura. Maybe Laura is just an object to me generally. Okay. But what about* Laura? *All of this seems to be saying that I'm the one with the problem. But what about* her *problem? What about* her *self-justifying images? Let's talk about* that!

My anger was building again, when all of a sudden I became aware of my anger. "Aware" is perhaps the wrong word. For I'm always aware, when I'm angry, that I'm angry. But this time I was aware of something more: I was aware of the *hypocrisy* in my anger. For here I was, angry that Laura was in the box, but in my anger at her being in the box, *I* was in the box. I was angry at her for being like I was being! The thought caught me short, and Laura seemed different to me in an instant—not different in the sense that she no longer had problems but different in the sense that I saw myself as having problems too. Her problems no longer seemed to excuse mine.

Kate's voice intruded on my thoughts. "Tom."

"Yeah?"

"Is this all making sense, Tom?"

"Yes. I understand it," I said slowly. "I don't necessarily *like* it, but I understand it." I paused, still thinking of Laura. "I think I have some work to do."

It was an interesting moment. For the first time that afternoon, I was fully open to what Bud and Kate were sharing with me—open to the possibility that I had a problem. More than open, actually. I *knew* I had a problem, and in some ways a big one. Until that moment, I'd felt giving in to the possibility that I had a problem would mean that I was the loser, that I'd been wrestled to the ground, that Laura had won. But now it didn't seem that way at all. I felt in a strange way free and unencumbered. Laura didn't win, and I didn't lose. The world seemed much different than it had the moment before. I felt hope. Imagine it! I felt hope in the moment I discovered I had a problem.

"I know what you mean," said Kate. "I have a lot of work to do myself."

"Me too," nodded Bud.

A moment or two passed in silence.

"We have one more thing to talk about," Bud said, "and then I want to turn our discussion back to business and see what all this means for Zagrum."

14   *Collusion*

"So far," he continued, "we've been examining the internal experience of someone who's in the box. But as you can imagine, my box can have quite an impact on others.

"Think about it," he said, walking to the board. "Suppose this is me—in my box," he said, drawing a box with a stick figure in it.

"If here I am in my box, what am I emitting?"

"What are you *emitting?*"

"I mean, what am I doing to others if I'm in the box toward them?"

"Oh," I said, searching my memory. "Well . . . you're blaming them, I guess."

"Right. So if I'm here in my box," he said, pointing to the diagram, "I'm blaming others." He drew an arrow pointing out to the right from his box. "But here's an important question: Are other people generally walking around saying to themselves, 'Gee, I really feel blameworthy today; I need someone to blame me'?"

I laughed. "Yeah, right."

"I don't think so either," Bud said. "Most people are generally walking around thinking something like, 'Look, I'm not perfect, but doggone it, I'm doing just about as well as you could expect under the circumstances.' And since most of us have self-justifying images we're carrying around with us, most people are already in a defensive posture, always ready to defend their self-justifying images against attack. So if I'm in the box, blaming others, my blame invites them to do— *what?*"

"I guess your blame would invite *them* to be in the box."

"Exactly," he said, drawing a second person in a box. "By blaming, I invite others to get in the box, and they then blame me for blaming them unjustly. But because, while I'm in the box, I feel justified in blaming them, I feel that *their* blame is unjust and blame them even more. But of course, while they're in the box they feel justified in blaming me and feel that my further blame is unjust. So they blame *me* even more. And so on. So, by being in the box, I invite others to be in the box in response," he said, adding more arrows between the boxes. "And others, by being in the box in response, invite me to *stay* in the box, like this."

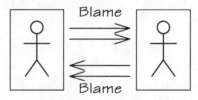

Bud then added a sixth sentence to the principles he was writing about self-betrayal:

"Self-betrayal"

1. An act contrary to what I feel I should do for another is called an act of "self-betrayal."
2. When I betray myself, I begin to see the world in a way that justifies my self-betrayal.

3. When I see a self-justifying world, my view
   of reality becomes distorted.
4. So—when I betray myself, I enter the box.
5. Over time, certain boxes become characteristic of me, and I carry them with me.
6. By being in the box, I provoke others to
   be in the box.

"You can put any flesh on these bones that you'd like," Kate added, pointing to the diagram, "and you'll see that when someone's in the box, the same self-provoking pattern always emerges. Let me give you an example.

"I have an 18-year-old son named Bryan. And to be frank, he's been a struggle. One of the things that really bugs me is that he frequently gets home late."

I'd been so caught up in thinking about Laura that I'd nearly forgotten my troubles with Todd. The mere thought of him now, in response to Kate's comment about her boy, darkened my mood.

"Now imagine that I'm in the box toward Bryan. If I am, how do you suppose I'd likely see him and his getting home late?"

"Well," I said, "you'd see him as irresponsible."

"Okay, good," said Kate. "How else?"

"You'd think he's a troublemaker."

"And disrespectful," added Bud.

"Yes," agreed Kate. Then pointing to the board, she asked, "Is it okay if I erase this blame diagram, Bud?"

"Sure."

She drew a summary of what we'd said. "Okay," she said, putting some finishing touches on a drawing. "So here we have it."

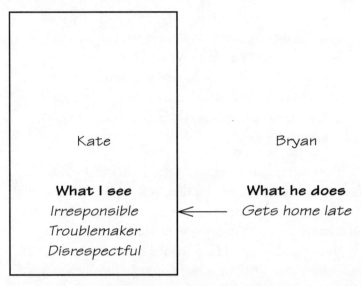

"Now if I'm in the box and see Bryan as an irresponsible and disrespectful troublemaker, what sorts of things do you suppose I might do in this situation?"

"Well—" I said, thinking.

"You'd probably discipline him pretty severely," Bud interjected.

"And you might start criticizing him a lot," I added.

"Okay, good," Kate said, adding to the drawing. "Anything else?"

"You'd probably start hovering over his shoulder to make sure he was staying out of trouble," I said.

She added that to the drawing and stepped to the side. "Now let's suppose Bryan betrays himself—that he's in the box toward *me*. If he's in the box toward me, how do you suppose he might see me and my disciplining, criticizing, and hovering over his shoulder?"

"He'd probably see you as dictatorial," I said. "Or maybe unloving."

"And nosey," Bud added.

"Okay, 'dictatorial,' 'unloving,' and 'nosey,'" she repeated as she added to the drawing. "Okay, good," she said. "Now look what we have."

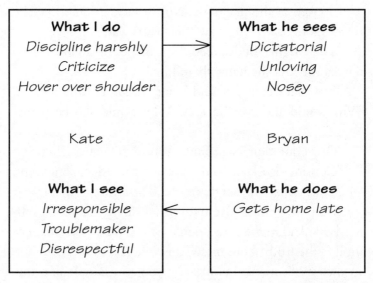

What I do		What he sees
Discipline harshly		*Dictatorial*
Criticize		*Unloving*
Hover over shoulder		*Nosey*
Kate		Bryan
What I see		**What he does**
Irresponsible		*Gets home late*
Troublemaker		
Disrespectful		

"If Bryan's in the box and seeing me as an unloving, nosey dictator, do you suppose he'll want to be home earlier or later?"

"Oh, later," I said. "*Far* later."

"In fact," Bud added, "he'll be less likely to do *anything* as you'd like him to do it."

"Yes," Kate agreed, drawing another arrow from Bryan's box to her own. "So around and around we go," she said, adding still more arrows between the boxes. "Think of it: we provoke each other to do more of what we say we don't like about the other!"

"Yeah, think about it, Tom," said Bud. "If you were to ask Kate in this situation what she wants more than anything else in the whole world, what do you suppose she would tell you?"

"That she wants Bryan to be more responsible, less trouble, and so on."

"Precisely. But what's the effect of what Kate does in the box? Does she invite more of what she says she wants?"

I looked at the diagram. "No. In fact, it looks like she invites more of what she says she *doesn't* want."

"That's right," Bud agreed. "She invites Bryan to do more of what she says she hates about him."

"But that's crazy," I said, after a moment's reflection. "Why would she ever do that? Why would she keep that going?"

"Great question," said Bud. "Why don't you ask her?"

"Consider it asked," said Kate. She paused for a moment, apparently collecting her thoughts. "The answer is that I can't see what I'm doing. Remember, I'm in the box—self-deceived. And in the box, I don't see clearly. In the box, I'm blind to the truth about myself and others. I'm even blind to my own motivations. Let me give you an example of something that happened in this situation to show what I mean.

"As you might have assumed, I've been in the box toward Bryan. Everything you said I'd probably do—discipline harshly, criticize, hover over his shoulder—I've done them all. But it's not so much *what* I've done that's been the problem but *the way I've been* when I've done it. I think that in some cases, discipline—even harsh discipline—is what a child might need. But my problem has been that when I disciplined Bryan, I wasn't doing it because of what Bryan needed. I was doing it because I was mad at how he was making my life difficult. So the problem with my disciplining, and so on, has been that I've been in the box when I've been doing it. I haven't been seeing my own son as a person to help but as an object to blame. And that's what he has felt and responded to.

"Well, on a Friday night in the middle of all this, about a year ago, he asked if he could use the car. I didn't want him to use it, so I gave him an insanely early curfew time as a condition—a time I didn't think he could accept. 'Okay, you can use it,' I said smugly, 'but only if you're back by 10:30.' 'Okay, Mom,' he said, as he whisked the keys off the key rack. The door banged behind him.

"I plopped myself down on the couch, feeling very burdened and vowing that I'd never let him use the car again. The whole evening went that way. The more I thought about it, the madder I got at my irresponsible kid.

"I remember watching the 10 o'clock news, stewing over Bryan the whole time. My husband, Steve, was home too. We were both complaining about Bryan when we heard the squeal of tires in the driveway. I looked at my watch. It was 10:29. And you know what?"

I was all ears.

"In that moment, when I saw the time, I felt a keen pang of disappointment."

"Now think about that for a minute," she continued after a short pause. "That night, I would have told you that the thing I wanted most was for Bryan to be responsible, to keep his word, to be trustworthy. But—when he actually *was* responsible, when he did what he said he'd do, when he proved himself trustworthy, was I happy?"

"No, you weren't," I said, beginning to think of the implications.

"That's right. And when he came bounding into the house and said, 'Made it, Mom,' what do you think I said? Do you think I patted him on the back and said 'Good job'?"

"No, you probably said 'Yeah, but you shouldn't have squealed the tires' or something like that."

"That's right. What I actually said was 'You sure cut it close, didn't you?' Notice — even when he *was* responsible, I couldn't *let* him be responsible."

"Wow, that's amazing," I said half under my breath, thinking of my own son, Todd.

"Yes. So is a responsible son what I really wanted most?"

"I guess not," I answered.

"That's right," she said. "When I'm in the box, there's something I need more than what I think I want most. It's like I said a couple of minutes ago. In the box, I'm blind even to my own motivations. So what do you think that is? What do I need most when I'm in the box?"

I repeated the question to myself. *What do I need most when I'm in the box? What do I need?* I wasn't sure.

Kate leaned toward me. *"What I need most when I'm in the box is to feel justified.* And if I'd spent my whole night, and really a lot longer than that, blaming my son, what do I need from my son in order to feel 'justified,' to feel 'right'?"

"You need him to be wrong," I said slowly, a knot forming in my stomach. "In order to be justified in blaming him, you need him to be blame*worthy*."

In that moment I was transported back some 16 years. I was handed a little bundle by the nurse, and from that bundle, two cloudy-gray eyes looked up in the direction of my face. I was completely unprepared for what he would look like at birth. Bruised, misshapen, and gray, he was a funny-looking kid, and I was his daddy.

I had been blaming Todd almost from that day. He was never smart enough, never coordinated enough. And he was always in the way. Since he started school he had been in constant trouble. I don't remember ever feeling proud when anyone realized he was my son. He'd never been good enough.

Kate's story scared me to death. I asked myself, *What must it be like to be the son of someone for whom you can never be good enough? And if Kate's right, then there's a sense in which I can't let him be good enough. I need him to be a problem in order to feel justified in always seeing him as a problem.* I felt sick, and I tried to push Todd out of my mind.

"That's exactly right," I heard Kate say. "Having spent the evening accusing Bryan of being a disappointment, I *needed* him to be a disappointment *so that I would be justified in accusing him.*"

We sat for a moment in thought.

Finally, Bud broke the silence. "This raises an astonishing point, Tom," he said. "When I'm in the box, I need people to cause trouble for me—*I need problems.*"

Yeah, I thought. *I guess that's right.*

Bud paused and then rose from his chair.

"Remember when you asked me this morning whether you can actually run a business being out of the box all the time? I think your point was that it seemed like you'd get run over if you were out of the box all the time, seeing people as people."

"Yeah, I remember."

"And then we talked about how that question is misguided since you can do almost any behavior—'soft,' 'hard,' whatever—either in the box or out of the box. Do you remember?"

"Yes."

"Well, now we can say more about your question. It's an important question. Let's apply what we've just learned to it.

Think of it this way: Who *needs* to be run over—the person who is *in* the box or the person who is *out?*"

"The person *in* the box," I said, amazed by the implication.

"That's right. Out of the box I get no mileage whatsoever in being run over. I don't need it. And what's more, I'm usually not doing anyone a favor by letting them run over me. *In* the box, on the other hand, I get what I most need when I'm run over: I get my justification. I get my proof that the person running over me is just as bad as I've been accusing him or her of being."

"But in the box, you don't *really* want to be run over, do you?" I asked. "I mean, that's kind of strange. Kate's story got me thinking about my son, Todd. Laura and I feel like we get run over sometimes, but I don't think either of us really *wants* that."

"That's true," Bud responded. "We're not saying that in the box we *enjoy* problems. Far from it. We hate them. In the box, it seems like there's nothing we would want more than to be out from under them. But remember, when we're in the box we're self-deceived—we're blind to the truth about others and ourselves. And one of the things we're blind to is how the box itself undercuts our every effort to obtain the outcomes we want. Let's go back to Kate's story and I'll show you what I mean."

Bud walked over to the board. "Remember," he said, pointing to Kate's diagram, "Kate would tell you in this situation that she wants Bryan to be respectful, responsible, and less of a troublemaker. And she'd be telling you the truth. She really *does* want that. But she's blind to how everything she does in the box actually provokes Bryan to be just the opposite. Notice—her blaming provokes Bryan to be irresponsible, and then, when he *is* irresponsible, she takes that as justification for having blamed him in the first place for being irresponsible! Likewise, Bryan's blaming provokes Kate to be on his case, and then, when she *is* on his case, he takes that as justification for having blamed her in the first place for being on his case! By the simple fact of being in the box, each helps create the very problems they blame the other for."

"In fact," Kate added, "Bryan and I provide each other with such perfect justification, it's almost as if we *colluded* to do so. It's as if we said to each other, 'Look, I'll mistreat you so you can blame your bad behavior on me if you'll mistreat me so I can blame my bad behavior on you.' Of course we didn't ever say that to each other, or even think it for that matter. But our mutual provocation and justification seem so perfectly coordinated, it *looks* like we did. For this reason, when two or more people are in their boxes toward each other, mutually betraying themselves, we often call it 'collusion.' And when we're in collusion, we actually collude in condemning ourselves to ongoing mutual mistreatment!"

"And we do this," Bud jumped back in, "not because we like being mistreated but because we're in the box, and the box *lives* on the justification it gets from our being mistreated. So there's a peculiar irony to being in the box: However bitterly I complain about someone's poor behavior toward me and about the trouble it causes me, I also find it strangely *delicious*. It's my proof that others are as blameworthy as I've claimed them to be—and that I'm as innocent as I claim *myself* to be. The behavior I complain about is the very behavior that justifies me."

Bud placed both hands on the table and leaned toward me. "So simply by being in the box," he said slowly and earnestly, "I provoke in others the very behavior I say I hate in them. And they then provoke in me the very behavior they say they hate in me."

Bud turned and added another sentence to the principles about self-betrayal:

"Self-betrayal"

1. An act contrary to what I feel I should do for another is called an act of "self-betrayal."
2. When I betray myself, I begin to see the world in a way that justifies my self-betrayal.
3. When I see a self-justifying world, my view of reality becomes distorted.
4. So—when I betray myself, I enter the box.
5. Over time, certain boxes become characteristic of me, and I carry them with me.
6. By being in the box, I provoke others to be in the box.
7. In the box, we invite mutual mistreatment and obtain mutual justification. We collude in giving each other reason to stay in the box.

"Once in the box," Bud said, backing away from the board, "we give each other reason to *stay* in the box. That's the grim reality."

"Pretty grim," I agreed, suddenly aching for my boy.

"Now look, Tom," Bud said, sitting back down in his chair. "Think about how self-betrayal, and everything we've been talking about, explains the self-deception problem—the problem of being unable to see that I have a problem. To begin with, when I'm in the box, who do I think has the problem?"

"Others."

"But when I'm in the box, who, in fact, has the problem?"

"You do," I answered.

"But what does my box provoke in others?" he asked.

"It provokes them to behave badly toward you."

"Yes. In other words, my box provokes *problems* in others. It provokes what I take as proof that I'm not the one with the problem."

"Yeah, that's right," I agreed.

"So what will I do if anyone tries to correct the problem they see in *me?*"

"You'll resist them," I answered.

"Exactly," he said. "When having a problem, I don't think I have one. I think *other* people are responsible." He paused for a moment, then said, "So here's the question: So what?"

So what? I repeated to myself. "What do you mean, 'So what?'"

"I mean just that," Bud answered. "Why should we care about any of this at Zagrum? What does it have to do with work?"

15 *Box Focus*

"Well it has *everything* to do with it," I said, surprised by the strength of my opinion.

"How?" Bud asked.

"How?" I replied.

"Yes, how?" Bud said with a slight smile.

"Well, to begin with," I said, "nearly everyone at work is in the box, as near as I can tell. At least nearly everyone at Tetrix was."

"So what?"

"So *what?*" I repeated.

"Yeah, so what?" he said.

"Well, if we're in the box, we'll be inviting others to be in the box as well, and we'll end up with all kinds of conflict that gets in the way of what we're trying to do."

"Which is what?" Bud asked.

"What do you mean, 'Which is what?' "

"You just said that all of that conflict would get in the way of what we're trying to do. So my question is, What is it we're trying to do?"

"Oh. Well, I guess we're trying to be productive."

"But why?"

"Why?" I was surprised by the question.

"Yes. Why are you trying to be productive? What's the *purpose* of productivity?"

"Oh . . . um . . . we're trying to be productive so that we can achieve the company's goals."

"Ah," Bud said, as though he had finally found something he had been looking for for a long time. "So you can achieve *results*."

"Yes, that's what I mean," I said, happy for the help.

"Let me ask you another question then."

"Okay," I said, by now feeling a bit like a baseball catcher who was having a difficult time with a knuckleballer.

"If the point of all our efforts at work is to achieve results, what's the effect of the box on our collective ability to do *that*?"

"Well, that's my point," I said. "We can't really achieve results like we otherwise could if we're in the box."

"Why not?" Bud asked.

This was starting to get ridiculous. "What do you mean, 'Why not?'" I asked, failing to conceal my irritation.

"That's what I mean," he responded, undaunted. "Why can't we achieve results like we otherwise could if we're in the box? Why does the box matter?"

"Well . . . it just . . . I mean . . . I mean, come on, *doesn't* it matter?" I said, finally.

"I don't know. That's why I'm asking."

I was entirely confused. I knew it mattered, but for the life of me I couldn't find an appropriate way to explain why.

"Think about it this way, Tom. When I'm in the box, who or what am I focused on?"

"On yourself, I guess," I answered.

"Exactly. Then let me ask again: What is it about the box that keeps me from focusing on results?"

All of a sudden the answer hit me. *"You can't focus on results because in the box you're focused on yourself."*

"Exactly, Tom. Exactly. When we're in the box, we can't focus on results. We're too busy focusing on ourselves instead. Even most of the people you've encountered in your career who you think are results-focused really aren't. They value results primarily for the purpose of creating or sustaining their own stellar reputations. And you can tell because they generally don't feel that other people's results are as important as their own. Think about it—most people aren't nearly so happy when other people in the organization succeed as they are when they themselves do. So they run all over people trying to get only their *own* results—with devastating effects. They might beat their chests and preach focusing on results, but it's a lie. In the box, they, like everyone else, are just focused on themselves. But in the box, they, like everyone else, can't see it."

"And it's even worse than that," Kate added. "Because, remember, in the box we provoke others to get in the box. We withhold information, for example, which gives others reason to do the same. We try to control others, which provokes the very resistance that we feel the need to control all the more. We withhold resources from others, who then feel the need to protect resources from us. We blame others for dragging their feet and in so doing give them reason to feel justified in dragging their feet all the more. And so on.

"And through it all we think that all our problems would be solved if Jack wouldn't do this or if Linda wouldn't do that or if XYZ department would just straighten up or if the company would get a clue. But it's a lie. It's a lie even if Jack, Linda, XYZ department, and the company *need* to improve, which they surely do. Because when I'm blaming them, I'm not doing it because they need to improve, I'm blaming them because their shortcomings justify *my* failure to improve.

"So," she continued, "one person in an organization, by being in the box and failing to focus on results, provokes his or her coworkers to fail to focus on results as well. Collusion spreads far and wide, and the end result is that coworkers position themselves against coworkers, workgroups against workgroups, departments against departments. People who came together to help an organization succeed actually end up delighting in each other's failures and resenting each other's successes."

"That's really crazy," I said in amazement. "But I see just what you're talking about all the time. Tetrix was full of those kinds of situations."

"Yes. Think about it," Bud said. "When were you most happy—when Chuck Staehli succeeded, or when he failed?"

The question caught me off guard. I had meant that I'd seen this in *others* all the time. Staehli *really was* a problem. I wasn't just making that up. And he created all kinds of trouble—conflict, poor teamwork, and so on. "I, uh, I . . . I don't know," I offered weakly.

"Well, you might think about it a little. When dealing with germs, one person's being sick doesn't mean that I'm *not* sick. In fact, when I'm surrounded by sick people, chances are greater that I will get sick myself."

He paused and looked at me for a moment. "Remember Semmelweis?"

"The doctor who discovered the cause of the high mortality rate in the maternity ward?"

"Yes. In his case, even the doctors spread the disease. And once they passed it on, others became carriers too—including the patients they came in contact with. Childbed fever, with its various symptoms, spread unchecked, claiming victim after victim. All because of a single germ no one knew about—most especially those who carried it. What happens in organizations is analogous."

Bud stood up and moved to the board. "Let me show you what I mean."

107

16 *Box Problems*

"Do you remember my experience in San Francisco?" Bud asked.

"Yeah."

"Remember the problems I had there? How I wasn't engaged, wasn't committed, and was making things more difficult for others?"

"Yeah, I remember."

Bud erased everything that had been written next to the self-betrayal diagram. Then he wrote the following:

Lack of commitment
Lack of engagement
Troublemaking

"Okay, here are a few of the problems I had in San Francisco," he said, as he stepped back from the board. "My 'symptoms,' as it were. But let's add as many kinds of problems to this list as we can. What are some other common people problems in organizations?"

"Conflict," I said. "Lack of motivation."

"Stress," Kate added.

"Poor teamwork," I said.

"Hold on a minute," said Bud, writing furiously. "I'm trying to get them all up here. Okay, go ahead. What else?"

"Backbiting, alignment problems, lack of trust," added Kate.

"Lack of accountability," I added. "Bad attitudes. Communication problems."

"Okay, good," Bud said, finishing the last few. "That's a good enough list. Now let's take a look and compare it to the story right over here where I failed to get up and tend to my child."

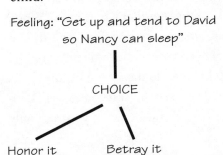

Feeling: "Get up and tend to David
so Nancy can sleep"

CHOICE

Honor it   Betray it
             "Self-betrayal"

How I started to see myself	How I started to see Nancy
Victim	Lazy
Hardworking	Inconsiderate
Important	Unappreciative
Fair	Insensitive
Sensitive	Faker
Good dad	Lousy mom
Good husband	Lousy wife

Lack of commitment
Lack of engagement
Troublemaking
Conflict
Lack of motivation
Stress
Poor teamwork
Backbiting/
  bad attitudes
Misalignment
Lack of trust
Lack of accountability
Communication
  problems

"Notice: Did I have a commitment or engagement problem after I betrayed myself?"

"Yes," I answered.

"But how about *before*? Did I have a commitment or engagement problem when I just had the feeling to get up and tend to David so Nancy could sleep?"

"No. Not at all," I said.

"How about making things more difficult for others? Was I making things more difficult for Nancy when I just had the feeling to help her?"

"No," I answered, "only after you betrayed yourself."

"That's right. And how about conflict—and stress? When do you suppose I was more stressed—when I just felt I should help Nancy or after I betrayed myself and was inflating the importance of the things I had to do the next morning?"

"Oh, after you betrayed yourself, for sure. Same with conflict. You felt no conflict before you betrayed yourself, only after."

"That's right," Bud agreed. "You can go down all of these people problems, and what you'll find is that they all existed after I betrayed myself but not before."

Bud paused, giving me a chance to look at the list and see for myself.

"Which means what?" he asked.

"I'm not sure I understand what you mean."

"Well, I had all of these people problems after I betrayed myself but not before. Which means what?"

"Which means . . . uh . . . *oh*. Which means that they were caused by your self-betrayal," I finally said.

"Exactly, Tom. I didn't have those problems before I betrayed myself, only after. So the solution to the self-betrayal problem *is* the solution to all of those people problems."

Bud paused again, giving me time to digest the idea.

"Remember how I said, Tom, that, like Semmelweis's medical discovery, the solution to the self-deception problem amounts to a sort of unifying theory—a theory that shows that the various disparate problems we call 'people problems' really all have the same cause?"

"Yeah, I remember."

"Well, here's what I meant. Right here," he said, pointing to the diagram. "This simple story shows how it happens. Self-betrayal is the germ that creates the disease of self-deception. And, like childbed fever, self-deception has many different symptoms—from lack of motivation and commitment to stress and communication problems. Organizations die, or are severely crippled, by those symptoms. And that happens because those who carry the germ don't know they're carrying it."

I thought about the import of that for a moment, studying the diagram. "But is it always the same in business?" I asked after a moment or two. "I mean, after all, your example is about failing to get up to tend to a baby. That's not what's happening at work."

"That's true," he said. "You're right that the people at work aren't betraying themselves quite this way—no one is failing to tend to a baby. However, a lot of people are failing to do things for coworkers that they feel they should do, and every time that happens, the same elements spin out just like in this example. Every time we betray ourselves, we go in the box, and it doesn't matter where we betray ourselves—whether at home, at work, at the store, wherever. And the box—self-deception—will itself cause all the same kinds of problems in every one of those situations that it caused in this one.

"But there's something else," Bud continued. "There's a particular, foundational self-betrayal that almost everyone shares at work. It has to do with what we were talking about a few minutes ago—our failure to do what we were hired to do, to focus on helping the organization and its people achieve results. The key to solving most of the people problems that afflict organizations will be in discovering how we can solve that foundational workplace self-betrayal."

"So how *do* you?" I asked eagerly.

"Ah, we're not quite ready to understand that yet. We have a few more ideas to consider first. But maybe we should take a break before we get to it."

Kate glanced at her watch. "I'm going to have to leave I'm afraid, guys. I have a 4:30 with Howard Chen. I wish I didn't have to."

"Tom," she said, rising from her chair and extending her hand to me. "It's been a real pleasure spending this time with you. I appreciate how seriously you're taking this. As I said before, there's nothing more important to us around here than what you're now learning. It's Zagrum's number one strategic initiative. You'll understand what that means as you get into what comes next."

"What do you think?" she said, turning to Bud. "Are you going to try to finish up the basics tonight?"

"If so, we'll be going a little late. Tom and I will have to talk about it."

"Sounds good," Kate said as she turned toward the door.

"By the way, Tom," she said, turning back to me. "I *left* Zagrum once. It was a very different company then."

"Why'd you leave?" I asked.

"Because of Lou Herbert."

That wasn't the answer I expected. "Really? I thought you and Lou were really tight."

"Not in the early days. Lou wasn't tight with anybody then. A lot of good people left."

"Then why'd you come back?"

"Because of Lou," she said.

I was confused. "What do you mean?"

"Lou found this material—the material you're learning now—and it transformed him. And in transforming *him*, it

112

transformed the company. When he flew out to meet me, he came to apologize, and he came with a plan. I've worked for Zagrum twice, but it might as well have been two different companies. You're learning about the need to apologize, like Lou. And you'll soon learn about the plan that follows from it. As I told you before, everything we do here is built on what you're learning. It's what makes this place tick."

She paused and touched her hand to my elbow. "We're glad you're part of the team, Tom. You wouldn't be here unless we believed in you."

"Thanks," I replied.

"And thank *you*, Bud," she said, turning his direction. "You never cease to amaze me."

"What are you talking about?" he asked, chuckling.

"I'm talking about what you mean to the company and the people in it. You're just like Lou became after he got his act together. You're Zagrum's secret weapon."

Kate smiled and turned toward the door. "Anyway, thanks," she said as she walked out. "And keep rooting for the Cardinals—both of you. Yes, even you, Bud," she said, responding to his frown. "Heaven knows, they need the help."

"Wow," I said to no one in particular, after she left. "I can't believe she took all that time to be with me today."

"Believe me," said Bud. "You don't know the half of it. She has tremendous demands on her time. But she comes whenever she can. And she comes because what we're now embarked on produces more results for this company than any other single thing we do. Her attendance is her way of saying 'We're serious about this. And if you aren't, you won't stay long.'

"Well, Tom," Bud said, signaling a change in topic, "we have a decision to make. We have a few more hours to go

113

before we're through with the basics. And we can either finish tonight or meet again tomorrow, if that's possible for you."

I thought about my schedule. I had a full afternoon but could clear my morning schedule. "I think I'd prefer tomorrow morning."

"Good enough. Let's say 8:00 A.M. And if I can arrange it, I might even have a surprise for you."

"A surprise?"

"Yeah. If we're lucky."

The warm August wind blew through my hair as I turned my convertible from Longridge Road east onto Merrit Parkway. I had a wife and son who needed some attention, perhaps even some apologies. I hardly knew where to begin. But I knew that Todd liked working on cars—an interest I had ridiculed whenever I could out of fear that "Tom Callum's boy" would grow up to be a mechanic. And I also knew that Laura hadn't had a meal prepared for her in months. I had to pick up items for a barbecue, and I was feeling the desire to learn a thing or two about tuning engines.

For the first time in years, I was in a hurry to get home.

PART III

How We Get OUT *of the Box*

17   *Lou*

It was 8:15 A.M., and Bud wasn't in the conference room yet. I was starting to wonder if I'd heard him correctly when the doors burst open and into the room walked an elderly gentleman.

"Tom Callum?" he said with a hearty smile, extending his hand.

"Yes."

"Glad to meet you. My name's Lou. Lou Herbert."

"Lou Herbert?" I said in astonishment.

I'd seen pictures of Lou and some old video, but his presence was so unexpected that I would've never recognized him without his introduction.

"Yes. Sorry for the shock. Bud's on his way. He's just checking on a couple of things for a meeting we have this afternoon."

I was dumbstruck. No words came to mind, so I just stood there nervously—like a first-time actor who had suddenly forgotten his lines.

"You're probably wondering what I'm doing here," he said.

"Well, *yes*, as a matter of fact."

"Bud called last night and asked if I could join you guys this morning. He wanted me to explain a few things about my history here. I was coming over today anyway for a meeting this afternoon. So here I am."

"Well, I don't know what to say. This is incredible to meet you. I've heard so much about you."

"I know. It's almost like I'm already dead, isn't it?" he said with a grin.

"Yeah, I guess it kind of is," I said, chuckling, before I knew what I was saying.

"Look, Tom, go ahead, sit. Bud asked me to get started with you before he gets here." He gestured toward a seat, "Please."

I sat in my familiar chair from the afternoon before, and Lou took the seat across from me.

"So how's it been going?"

"You mean yesterday?"

"Yes."

"It was quite an amazing day, actually. Quite amazing."

"*Really?* Tell me about it," he said.

Although I'd been with Lou for only a minute or two, my nervousness had evaporated. His kindly eyes and gentle demeanor reminded me of my dad, who had died 10 years earlier. I felt completely comfortable in his presence and found myself wanting to share my thoughts with him as I used to with my father.

"Well," I said, "I hardly know where to begin. I learned a lot yesterday. But let me start with my boy."

Over the next fifteen minutes or so, I told Lou about the best night I'd had with Laura and Todd in at least five years. It was a night that was extraordinary only because I simply enjoyed being with them without there having to be anything extraordinary to make me enjoy it. I cooked, I laughed, I had my son teach me how to tune up the car. For the first time in I don't know how long, I enjoyed and felt grateful for my family. And for the first time in a long time, I went to bed with no hard feelings toward anyone in my home.

"What did Laura think of it all?" Lou asked.

"I don't think she knew what to think. She kept asking me what was going on until I finally had to tell her about what I learned yesterday."

"Oh, so you tried to teach her?"

"Yeah, and it was a disaster. I think it took me only a minute or so to have her thoroughly confused. 'The box,' 'self-betrayal,' 'collusion'—I butchered the ideas so badly, I couldn't believe it."

Lou smiled knowingly. "I know what you mean. You hear someone like Bud explain all this and it seems like the simplest thing in the world, but try to do it yourself and you quickly realize how subtle this all is."

"That's true. I think my explanations probably created more questions than they answered. But she listened and tried to understand anyway."

Lou listened intently, his eyes creased with kindness. And although I couldn't be sure, I thought I saw approval in them as well.

"You might check with Bud to see if this is still going on," Lou said, "but in the past, a couple of times a year we put on evening-long training events where interested family members could come and learn these ideas. It used to mean a lot to everybody that the company would do that for them. I'm sure it's still going on—you ought to check with Bud. Laura might really like it."

"Thanks. I'll check, for sure."

Just then, the door swung open and in walked Bud.

"Tom," he said, exasperated, "sorry I'm late. I had a few last-minute preparations for the meeting with the Klofhausen group this afternoon. As usual, there aren't enough last minutes." He set his briefcase down and took the seat between Lou and me at the head of the table.

"Well, Tom, we got lucky."

"What do you mean?"

"I mean Lou—he's the surprise I was hoping for. Lou's story is the story of how this material has transformed Zagrum, and I wanted him to share it with you if he could."

"Well, I'm happy I can be here," Lou said graciously. "But before we get into that story, Bud, I think you should hear about Tom's night last night."

"Oh, yes, Tom, I'm sorry. Tell me about your evening."

I don't know why, perhaps because I work for Bud and wanted badly to impress him, but I was reticent at first to share what I had shared with Lou. But Lou kept prodding me— 'Tell him about this,' or 'Tell him about that'—and I soon relaxed and told Bud all about my evening. After 10 minutes or so, he was smiling, just as Lou had been.

"That's terrific, Tom," Bud said. "How was Todd through the evening?"

"About the same as usual—pretty silent. He basically responded to my questions as he always does—mostly with 'yes's,' 'no's' and 'I don't know's.' But I didn't seem to mind it last night, whereas before it would've driven me crazy."

"That reminds me of *my* boy," Lou said, looking past me and out the window.

He paused for a moment, his eyes looking far away, as if retrieving something from the distant past. "The story of Zagrum's turnaround starts with him."

18   *Leadership in the Box*

"My youngest boy, Cory, who's now almost 40, was a handful. Drugs, drinking—you name it, he did it. Everything came to a head when he was arrested for selling drugs during his senior year in high school.

"At first I wanted to deny it. No Herbert ever did drugs. And to sell them—that was unthinkable. I stomped around demanding that this injustice be exposed. It couldn't be true. Not about *my* boy. So I demanded a full trial. Our lawyer recommended against it, and the district attorney offered a plea bargain that included only 30 days in jail. But I wouldn't have it. 'I'll be damned if my son is ever going to go to jail,' I said. And so we fought.

"But we lost, and Cory ended up spending a full year in the youth detention facility up in Bridgeport. As far as I was concerned, it was a blight on the family name. I visited him twice the whole year.

"When he got home, we hardly spoke. I rarely asked him anything, and when I did, he responded with barely audible one-word answers. He fell back into the wrong crowd, and within three months he'd been arrested again—this time for shoplifting.

"I wanted to deal with this one quietly. I had no illusions that he was innocent, so I pushed for a plea bargain that involved a 90-day wilderness treatment and survival program in the high country of Arizona. Five days later, I boarded a plane, Cory in tow, from JFK to Phoenix. I was taking him to be 'fixed.'

"My wife, Carol, and I dropped him off at the organization's headquarters. We watched as he was loaded into a white Suburban with other kids who were entering the program, and away they drove toward the mountains of eastern central Arizona. We were then escorted into a room for an all-day session—a session where I expected to learn how the people there were going to fix my son.

"But that's not what I learned. I learned that whatever my son's problems might be, *I* needed fixing too. What I learned changed my life. Not at first, for I fought everything they were suggesting tooth and nail: 'What, *me?*' I protested. '*I* don't do drugs. *I'm* not the one who spent most of my senior year in high school behind bars. *I'm* not the thief. I'm a responsible person—respected, the president of a company even.' But gradually I came to see the lie in my defensiveness. I came to discover, in a way I can describe only as simultaneously painful and hopeful, that I had been, for years, in the box toward my wife and my kids."

"In the box?" I said quietly, almost under my breath.

"Yes. In the box," Lou responded. "I learned that first day in Arizona what you learned yesterday. And in that moment—about the time when my son was probably climbing out of the Suburban and looking around at the isolated wilderness that would be his home for the next three months—I felt for the first time in years an overwhelming desire to take him in my arms and hold him. What desperate loneliness and shame he must be feeling. And how I had added to it! His last hours—or, for that matter, months and maybe even years—with his dad were spent under a silent cloud of blame. It was all I could do to hold back the tears.

"But it was worse than that. That day I realized that my box had driven away not only my son but also the most important people in my company. Two weeks earlier, in what people around the company were calling the 'March Meltdown,' five of the six executive team members left for 'better opportunities.'"

"Kate?" I asked.

"Yes. Kate was one of them."

Lou stared intently into nowhere, apparently in deep thought.

"It's amazing when I think back on it now," he said finally. "I felt betrayed by them the same way I felt betrayed by Cory. *To hell with them*, I told myself. *To hell with them all*.

"I was determined," he continued, "to build Zagrum into a success without them. *They weren't that great anyway*, I told myself. They'd been around, most of them, for the full six or so years since I'd purchased the company from John Zagrum, and the company was basically limping along. *If they were any good, we'd be doing better by now*, I thought. *To hell with them*.

"But it was a lie. Now it might've been true that we should've been doing better. But it was still a lie—because I was completely blind to my own role in our mediocrity. And as a result, I was blind to how I was blaming them *not* for *their* mistakes, but for *mine*. I was blind, as we always are, to my own box.

"But I recovered my sight in Arizona. I saw in myself a leader who was so sure of the brilliance of his own ideas that he couldn't allow brilliance in anyone else's, a leader who felt he was so 'enlightened' that he needed to see workers negatively in order to prove his enlightenment, a leader so driven to be the best that he made sure no one else could be as good as he was."

Lou paused. "You've learned about collusion, haven't you, Tom?"

"Where two people are both in their boxes toward each other? Yes."

"Well, with self-justifying images that tell me that I'm brilliant, enlightened, and the best, you can imagine the collusions I was provoking around here. In the box, I was a walking excuse factory—both for myself and for others. Any workers who needed the slightest justification for their own self-betrayals had a smorgasbord of options in me.

"I couldn't see, for example, that the more I took responsibility for my team's performance, the more mistrusted they felt. They then resisted in all kinds of ways: Some just gave up and left all creativity to me, others defied me and did things their own way, and still others left the company altogether. All of these responses convinced me all the more of the incompetence of the people in the company, so I responded by issuing even more careful instructions, developing even more policies and procedures, and so on. Everyone then took all that to be further evidence of my disrespect for them and resisted me all the more. And so on, round and round—each of us inviting the other to be in the box and in so doing providing each other with mutual justification for *staying* there. Collusion was everywhere. We were a mess."

"Just like Semmelweis," I said in amazement, under my breath.

"Oh, so Bud told you about Semmelweis?" Lou asked, looking at Bud and then back at me.

"Yes," I said, nodding along with Bud.

"Well, that's right," Lou continued. "The Semmelweis story is an interesting parallel. I was, in effect, killing the people in my company. Our turnover rate rivaled the mortality rate at Vienna General. I was carrying the disease I blamed everyone else for. I infected them and then blamed them for the infection. Our organizational chart was a chart of colluding boxes. We were a mess.

"But what I learned in Arizona was that *I* was a mess. Because I was in the box, I was provoking the very problems I was complaining about. I had chased away the very best people I knew—feeling justified all the time because in my box I was convinced they weren't that good."

Lou paused. "Even Kate," he added, shaking his head. "No one on this planet is any more talented than Kate, but I couldn't see that because of my box."

"So as I sat there in Arizona, I had a huge problem. I was sitting next to a wife whom I'd been taking for granted for 25 years. I was by then 100 miles of impassable terrain away from a son whose only recent memories of his father were probably bitter ones. And my company had come unglued—the best and brightest scattering around the globe, embarking on new careers. I was a lonely man. My box was destroying everything I cared about.

"One question seemed more important to me in that moment than anything else in the world: How can I possibly get out of the box?"

Lou paused, and I waited for him to continue.

"So how *do* you," I finally interjected. "How *do* you get out of the box?"

"You already know."

19 *Toward Being out of the Box*

"I do?" I searched my memory about the sessions the day before. I was sure we hadn't talked about it.

"Yes. And so did I when I was wondering how to get out."

"Huh?" At that moment I was really lost.

"Think about it. As I sat there regretting how I'd acted toward my wife, my son, and my coworkers, what were they to me? In that moment, was I seeing them as people or as objects?"

"In that moment, they were people to you," I said, my voice trailing off in thought.

"Yes. My blame, resentment, and indifference were gone. I was seeing them as they were, and I was regretting having treated them as *less* than that. So in that moment, where was I?"

"You were out of the box," I said softly, almost trancelike, trying to locate what made the change possible. I was feeling a bit like a spectator at a magic show who sees the rabbit surely enough but has no idea where it came from.

"Exactly. In the moment I felt the keen desire to be out of the box for them, I was *already* out of the box toward them. To feel that desire for them *is* to be out of the box toward them.

"And the same goes for you," he continued. "Think about your night last night with your family. What were they to you last night? Were you seeing them as people or as objects?"

"They were people," I said, amazed by the discovery.

"So if last night you were out of the box," Lou said, "then you already know how to get out of the box."

"But I don't," I said in protest. "I have no idea how it happened. In fact, I didn't even know I was out of the box last night until you just pointed it out to me. I couldn't begin to tell you how I got out."

"Yes you can. In fact, you already did."

"What do you mean?" I was completely bewildered.

"I mean, you told us about yesterday and about your night last night, about how you went home and spent the evening with your family. That story teaches us how to get out of the box."

"But that's my point. I don't see it."

"And this is my point: Yes you do. You just don't realize it yet. But you will."

That gave me a little bit of comfort, but not much.

"You see," Lou continued, "the question 'How do I get out of the box?' is really two questions. The first question is 'How do I *get* out?' and the second is 'How do I *stay* out once I'm out?' The question you're really worried about, I think, is the second—how you stay out. Think about it—I want to emphasize this again—when you're feeling that you want to be out of the box for someone, in that moment you're already out. You're feeling that way *because* you're now seeing him or her as a person. In feeling that way toward that person, you're *already* out of the box. So in that moment—like the moment you're having right now and like last night—when you're seeing and feeling clearly and want to be out of the box for others, what you're really asking is this: 'What can I do to *stay* out of the box toward them? What can I do to sustain the change I'm now feeling?' That's the question. And there are some pretty specific things we can do, once we're out of the box, to *stay* out of the box—and particularly for our purposes, in the workplace."

As Lou was talking, I started to understand what he meant. "Okay. I see how in feeling like I want to be out of the box for someone, in that moment I'm seeing him or her as a person, so in having that feeling I'm *already* out of the box toward that person. I understand that. And I understand how once I *am* out of the box, the question then is how to *stay* out—and I definitely want to get into that. Especially as applied to work. But I'm still scratching my head over how I got out in the first place—how my resentment toward Laura and Todd suddenly disappeared. Maybe I just got lucky last night. When I'm not so lucky, I'd like to know how to get myself out."

"Okay," Lou said, standing up. "Fair enough. I'll do my best, with Bud's help, to explain how we get out in the first place."

20 *Dead Ends*

"To begin with," Lou continued, "it helps to understand how we *don't* get out of the box."

He turned to the board and wrote: "What doesn't work in the box."

"To begin with," he said, turning back to me, "think about the things we try to do when we're in the box. For example, in the box, who do we think has the problem?"

"Others," I answered.

"That's right," he said, "so normally we spend a lot of energy in the box trying to change others. But does that work? Does that get us out of the box?"

"No."

"Why not?" he asked.

"Well, because that's the problem in the first place," I said. "I'm trying to change them because, in the box, I think they need to be changed. And that's the problem."

"But does that mean no one needs to be changed?" Lou asked. "Is everyone doing things just perfectly then? Is that what you're saying—that no one needs to *improve?*"

I felt a little stupid when he asked the question. *Come on, Callum,* I said to myself. *Think!* I wasn't being careful enough. "No, of course not. Everyone needs to improve."

"Well, then," he said, "why not the *other* guy? What's wrong if I want *him* to improve?"

That was a good question. *What is wrong with that?* I asked myself. I thought that's what all this meant, but at that moment I wasn't so sure. "I'm not sure," I said.

"Well, think about it this way. While it's true that others may have problems they need to solve, are *their* problems the reason I'm in the box?"

"No," I said. "That's what you think in the box, but it's a misperception."

"Exactly," said Lou. "So even if I were successful and the person I tried to change actually changed, would that solve the problem of my being in the box?"

"No, I guess it wouldn't."

"That's right, it wouldn't—even if the other person actually *did* change."

"And it's even worse than that," Bud interjected. "Think about what we talked about yesterday regarding collusion: When I'm in the box and try to get others to change, do I invite them to change as I'd like?"

"No," I said. "You'll end up provoking just the opposite."

"Exactly," Bud said. "My box ends up provoking more of the very thing I set out to change. So if I try to get out by changing others, I'll end up provoking others to give me reason to *stay* in the box."

"So," Lou said, turning to the board and writing, "trying to change others doesn't work."

What doesn't work in the box

1. Trying to change others

"What about doing my best to *cope* with others?" Lou said, turning from the board. "Does that work?"

"I wouldn't think so," I said. "That's essentially what I usually do. But it doesn't seem to get me out."

"That's right, it doesn't," Lou agreed. "And there's a simple reason why. 'Coping' has the same deficiency as trying to change the other person: It's just another way to continue blaming. It communicates the blame of my box, which just invites those I'm coping with to be in *their* box."

He turned to the board and added "coping" to the list of things that don't work.

What doesn't work in the box

1. Trying to change others
2. Doing my best to "cope" with others

"How about this one?" Bud added, while Lou was writing. "Leaving. Does leaving work? Will that get you out of the box?"

"Maybe," I said. "It seems like it might sometimes."

"Well, let's think about it. Where do I think the problem is when I'm in the box?"

"In others," I said.

"Exactly. But where *in fact* is the problem when I'm in the box?"

"In yourself."

"Yes. So if I leave, what goes with me?" he asked.

"The problem," I said softly, nodding. "I get it. The box goes with you."

"That's right," Bud said. "In the box, leaving is just another way to blame. It's just a continuation of my box. I take my lying feelings with me. Now it may be that in certain situations leaving is the right thing to do. But leaving a situation will never be sufficient, even if right. Ultimately, I have to leave my box too."

"Yeah, that makes sense," I said.

"Here, let me add that to the list," Lou said.

What doesn't work in the box
1. Trying to change others
2. Doing my best to "cope" with others
3. Leaving

"Here's another one to consider," said Lou. "How about communicating? Will that work? Will that get me out of the box?"

"Well it *seems* like it would," I said. "I mean, if you can't communicate, you don't have anything."

"Okay," said Lou, "let's consider this one carefully." He looked at the board. "Whose story is this over here about self-betrayal—is it yours, Bud?"

"Yes," Bud nodded.

"Oh yes, I see Nancy's name there," said Lou. "Okay, let's think about it. Look here, Tom, at Bud's story. After he betrayed himself, here's how he saw Nancy—as lazy, inconsiderate, insensitive, and so on. Now here's the question. If he tries to communicate with Nancy now, while he's in his box, what's he going to communicate?"

"Oh," I said, surprised by the implication. "He's going to communicate what he's feeling about her—namely, that she's all of those bad things."

"Exactly. And will that help? Is Bud likely to get out of the box by telling his wife that she's all the lousy things he's thinking she is when he's in the box?"

"No," I said. "But what if he's a little more sophisticated than that? I mean, with a little skill, he might be able to communicate more subtly and not just come right out and blast away."

"That's true," Lou agreed. "But remember, if Bud's in the box, then he's blaming. It's true he may be able to acquire some skills that would improve his communication techniques, but do you suppose those skills would hide his blame?"

"No, I suppose not," I said.

"That's the way it seems to me too," agreed Lou. "In the box, whether I'm a skilled communicator or not, I end up communicating my box—and that's the problem."

He turned and added "communicating" to the list.

What doesn't work in the box

1. Trying to change others
2. Doing my best to "cope" with others
3. Leaving
4. Communicating

"In fact," he added, backing away from the board, "this point about skills applies to skills generally, not just to communication skills. You might think about it this way: No matter what skill you teach me, I can be either *in* the box or *out* of the box when I implement it. And that raises this question: Will using a skill *in* the box be the way to get *out* of the box?"

"No," I said, "I guess not."

"That's why skill training in nontechnical areas often has so little lasting impact," Lou continued. "Helpful skills and techniques aren't helpful if they're done in the box. They just provide people with more sophisticated ways to blame."

"And remember, Tom," added Bud, "the people problems that most people try to correct with skills aren't due to a lack of skill at all. They're due to self-betrayal. People problems seem intractable not because they are insoluble but because the common skill interventions are not themselves solutions."

"That's exactly right," agreed Lou. "So," he said, turning and writing again, "we can't get out of the box simply by implementing new skills and techniques either."

What doesn't work in the box

1. Trying to change others
2. Doing my best to "cope" with others
3. Leaving
4. Communicating
5. Implementing new skills or techniques

I looked at the board and suddenly felt depressed. *What is left?* I thought.

"There's one more possibility we should consider," said Bud. "Here it is: What if I try to change *myself—my behavior?* Can that get me out of the box?"

"It looks like that's the only thing that *can* get you out," I answered.

"Let's consider it," said Bud, standing up and starting to pace. "This is tricky, but quite important. Let's think back to a couple of the stories we talked about yesterday.

"Remember the situation I told you yesterday about Gabe and Leon over in Building 6?"

I searched my memory but couldn't remember. "I'm not sure."

"Remember—Gabe had tried doing all kinds of things to let Leon know he was concerned about him?"

"Oh yeah, I remember."

"Well," he continued, "Gabe had changed his behavior toward Leon dramatically. But did that work?"

"No."

"And why not?"

134

"Because, as I recall, Gabe didn't really care about Leon, and that's what Leon understood through all of Gabe's outward changes."

"Exactly. Since Gabe was in the box toward Leon, every new thing Gabe tried to do from within his box just amounted to a change within the box. Leon remained an object to him through all his efforts.

"Think about that," Bud said, with emphasis. "Every new thing Gabe tried to do from within his box just amounted to a change within the box."

Bud took his seat. "Or think about the story where Nancy and I were arguing but I tried to apologize and put an end to it. Do you remember?"

I nodded, "Yeah."

"Well, it's the same thing," Bud said. "I changed myself in a radical way in that case: I changed all the way from arguing to kissing. But did that change get me out of the box?"

"No, because you didn't really mean it," I answered. "You were still *in* the box."

"Exactly. And that's just the point," Bud said, leaning toward me. "Because I was in the box, I *couldn't* mean it. In the box, every change I can think of is just a change in my style of being in the box. I can change from arguing to kissing. I can change from ignoring someone to going out of my way to shower that person with attention. But whatever changes I think of in the box are changes I think of from *within* the box, and they are therefore just more *of* the box—which is the problem in the first place. Others remain objects to me."

"That's right," Lou agreed, moving to the board. "So consider the implication, Tom. I can't get out of the box merely by changing my behavior either."

What doesn't work in the box
1. Trying to change others
2. Doing my best to "cope" with others
3. Leaving
4. Communicating
5. Implementing new skills or techniques
6. Changing my behavior

"But wait a minute," I said. "How is it possible to get out of the box at all, then? I mean, are you telling me that if I'm in the box and try to get out of the box, I won't be able to do it? That all of my efforts will just be newly styled efforts within the box and will therefore fail?"

"That's what we're saying," said Bud.

"But, come on, Bud, that can't be right. You're telling me that I can't get out by trying to change others or by doing my best to cope with others or by leaving, communicating, or implementing new skills and techniques. And then you're telling me on top of that that I can't even get out of the box by changing *myself?*"

"Well you can't get out by continuing to *focus on yourself*—which is what you do when you try to change your behavior in the box. So yes, that *is* what we're saying," he answered calmly.

"But then how could we *ever* get out? I mean, if what you're saying is right, then there's no way out. We're all stuck."

"Actually," Lou interjected. "That's not quite right. There *is* a way out, but it's different than anyone generally supposes. And you know what it is, just like I told you before. You just don't realize that you know it."

I was listening intently. I wanted to understand this.

"You were out of the box last night toward your family, right?"

"I guess so."

"Well, it sounded by the way you told your story like you were," Lou continued. "That means there *is* a way out. So let's think of your experience last night. Did you try to change your wife and son last night?"

"No."

"Did you feel like you were 'coping' with them?"

"No."

"And obviously you didn't leave. How about communicating? Did you get out because you communicated?"

"Well, maybe. I mean, we communicated very well—the best we'd done in a long time."

"Yes," Lou agreed, "but did you get out of the box because you communicated, or did you communicate well because you were out of the box?"

"Let me think," I said, more puzzled than ever. "I was already out of the box—I was out of box on my way home. Communicating isn't what *got* me out, I guess."

"Okay, then how about this last one?" Lou said, pointing at the list. "Did you get out of the box because you focused on and tried to change *yourself?*"

I sat there wondering, *What happened to me yesterday?* It ended in a magnificent evening, but I suddenly had no idea how I had gotten there. It was like I'd been abducted by aliens. *Did I set out to change myself?* That wasn't my memory. It felt more like something changed me. At least, I couldn't remember setting out to change. In fact, if anything, it seemed that along the whole way, I *resisted* the suggestion that I had to change. *So what happened? How did I get out of the box? Why did my feelings change?*

"I'm not sure," I said finally. "But I don't remember trying to change myself. Somehow, I just ended up changed—almost like something changed me. But I'm clueless as to how it happened."

"Here's something that might help you figure it out," Bud said. "Remember how when we started yesterday, we talked about how the distinction between being in the box and being out of the box is deeper than behavior?"

"Yeah, I remember that," I said.

"And we discussed the airplane-seating story, drew that diagram with behaviors up on top, and talked about how we can do almost any behavior in one of those two ways—either out of the box or in the box. Remember?"

"Yes."

"So consider this: If being in or out of the box is something that's deeper than behavior, do you suppose the key to getting out of the box will be a behavior?"

I started to see what he was saying. "No, I guess it wouldn't," I said, suddenly feeling hopeful that this thought would lead me to the answer.

"That's right," Bud said. "One of the reasons you may be struggling to understand how you got out of the box is that you're trying to identify a *behavior* that got you out. But since the box itself is deeper than behavior, the way out of the box has to be deeper than behavior too. Almost any behavior can be done either in the box or out of the box, so no mere behavior can get you out. You're looking in the wrong place."

"In other words," Lou interjected, "there's a fundamental problem with the question 'What do I need to *do* to get out of the box?' The problem is that anything I tell you to do can be done either *in* or *out of* the box. And if done in the box, that 'in-the-box' behavior can't be the way to get out. So you might then be tempted to say, 'Well, the answer, then, is to do that behavior out of the box.' Fair enough. But if you're out of the box, then you won't need the behavior anymore to *get* you out. Either way, the behavior isn't what gets you out. It's something else."

"But *what?*" I pleaded.

"Something right in front of you."

21 *The Way Out*

"Think about yesterday," Lou continued. "You just said that it felt like something changed you. We need to think about that a little more carefully."

Lou moved toward the board. "I want to talk about self-betrayal and the box for a moment—to make something clear that may not have been made explicit yet."

He drew the following diagram:

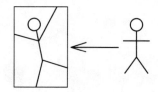

"To begin with, here's a picture of what life is like in the box," he said, pointing at his drawing. "The box is a metaphor for how I'm *resisting* others. By 'resisting,' I mean that my self-betrayal isn't passive. In the box, I'm actively resisting what the humanity of others calls me to do for them.

"For example," he said, pointing to Bud's story on the board, "Bud's story here about failing to get up so that Nancy could sleep—that initial feeling was an impression he had of something he should do for Nancy. He betrayed himself when he *resisted* that sense of what he should do for her, and in resisting that sense, he began to focus on himself and see her as being undeserving of help. His self-deception—his 'box'—is something he created and sustained through his active resistance of Nancy. This is why it's futile, as Bud was saying a few minutes ago, to try to get out of the box by focusing on ourselves: In the box, everything we think and feel is part of the lie of the box. The truth is, we change in the moment we cease resisting what is *outside* our box—others. Does that make sense?"

"Yeah, I think so."

"In the moment we cease resisting others, we're out of the box—liberated from self-justifying thoughts and feelings. This is why the way out of the box is always right before our eyes—*because the people we're resisting are right before our eyes.* We can stop betraying ourselves toward them—we can stop *resisting* them."

"But what can help me to do *that?*" I asked.

Lou looked at me thoughtfully. "There's something else you should understand about self-betrayal—something that may give you the leverage you're looking for.

"Think about your experience yesterday with Bud and Kate. How would you characterize it? Would you say that you were basically *in* or *out of* the box toward them?"

"Oh, *out*, for sure," I said. "At least most of the time," I added, giving Bud a sheepish grin. He smiled in return.

"But you've also indicated that you were *in* the box toward Laura yesterday. So there is a sense in which you were both in *and* out of the box at the same time—in the box toward Laura but out of the box toward Bud and Kate."

"Yeah, I guess that's right."

"This is an important point, Tom. Toward any one person or group of people, I'm either in or out of the box at any given moment. But since there are many people in my life—some toward whom I may be in the box more so than toward others—in an important sense I can be both in *and* out of the box at the same time. In toward some and out toward others.

"This simple fact can give us leverage to get out of the box in the areas of our lives where we may be struggling. In fact, that's what happened to you yesterday. Let me show you what I mean."

Lou walked to the board and modified his drawing.

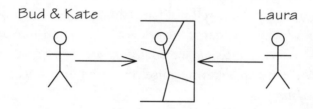

"Here's how we might depict what you were like yesterday," he said, standing to the side of the board. "You were in the box toward Laura but out of the box as you engaged with Bud and Kate. Now notice: Although you were resistant to Laura's needs because you were in the box toward her, you nevertheless retained a sense of what people generally might need because you were out of the box toward others — namely, Bud and Kate. This sense that you felt and honored toward Bud and Kate, combined with the continual call of Laura's humanity to you — which is always there — is what made getting out of the box toward Laura possible.

"So although it's true that there is nothing we can do from within the box to get ourselves out, in the out-of-the-box moments provided by our out-of-the-box relationships, there are a whole host of things we can do — things that can help us reduce our in-the-box moments and heal our in-the-box relationships. In fact, this is precisely what your experience with Bud and Kate did for you yesterday — you did something while you were out of the box toward Bud and Kate that helped you to get out of the box toward Laura."

My mind searched for the answer. "What did I do?"

"You questioned your own virtue."

"I what?"

"You questioned your own virtue. While you were *out* of the box, you listened to what Bud and Kate taught you about being *in* the box. And then you applied it to your own personal situations. The out-of-the-box nature of your experience with Bud and Kate invited you to do something that we never do in the box—it invited you to question whether you were in fact as out of the box as you had assumed in other areas of your life. And what you learned transformed your view of Laura.

"Now that probably didn't happen right off the bat," he continued, "but I'd bet there was a moment when it was like the light came pouring in—a moment when your blaming emotions toward Laura seemed to evaporate, and she suddenly seemed different to you than she had the moment before."

That was exactly how it happened, I thought to myself. I remembered that moment—when I saw the hypocrisy in my anger. It was as if everything changed in an instant. "That's true," I said. "That's what happened."

"Then we need to modify this drawing still more," Lou said, turning to the board.

Backing away from the board, he said, "This is how you looked when you left last night."

Bud & Kate   Tom   Laura

"You were seeing and feeling straightforwardly. Laura seemed different to you because in the moment you got out of the box toward her, you no longer had the need to blame her and inflate her faults.

"Now, in a way," he continued, "this is quite a miraculous thing. But in another way, it's the most common thing in the world. It happens all the time in our lives—usually on very small matters that are quickly forgotten. All of a sudden, because of the basic 'otherness' of the people who continually stand before us, *and* because of what we know as we stand out of the box in relation to other people, our box is penetrated by the humanity of others. We know in that moment what we need to do—we need to honor them as *people*. And in that moment—the moment I see another as a person, with needs, hopes, and worries as real and legitimate as my own— I'm out of the box."

"You might think about it this way," Bud interjected. "Look again at this story," he said, pointing to the diagram of his baby-crying story. "Once I have a feeling of something I should do to help another, where am I on this diagram?"

I looked at the board. "You're at the top again—back at the feeling."

"Exactly. I'm back out of the box. I can now choose the other way. I can now choose to honor that sense rather than betray it. And that, Tom, is the key to *staying* out of the box."

"In fact, Tom," Lou added, "I bet you had a feeling as you left here yesterday that there were some things you needed to do for some people last night. Am I right?"

"Yes," I said.

"And you did them, didn't you?" Lou asked.

"Yes, I did."

144

"That's why your night went as it did," he said. "You got out of the box toward Laura, and Todd for that matter, during your time with Bud and Kate. But your night went well because you *stayed* out of the box by doing for them what you felt you should do."

What Lou said seemed to explain my night with Laura and Todd well enough, but it left me feeling a little confused and overwhelmed about situations in general. How could people be expected to do everything they felt they should do for others? That didn't seem right.

"Are you saying that in order to stay out of the box, I have to always be doing things for others?"

Lou smiled, as if he'd been expecting me to ask. "That's an important question, Tom. We need to consider it with some care — maybe with a specific example." He paused for a moment, apparently thinking. "Let's think about driving. What would you say is your standard attitude toward other drivers on the road?"

I smiled to myself as I recalled a number of characteristic commutes. I remembered waving my fist at a driver who wouldn't slow down to let me merge, only to discover, after I'd forced my way in, that he was my neighbor. And I remembered glaring at the driver of a maddeningly slow car as I sped around him, only to discover, to my horror, that he was the same neighbor. "I suppose I'm pretty indifferent toward them," I chuckled, unable to suppress my amusement. "Unless, of course, they're in my way."

"It sounds like we went to the same driving school," Lou said, returning the smile. "But you know what? Occasionally I've had very different feelings toward other drivers. For example, it sometimes occurs to me that each of these people on the road is just as busy as I am and just as wrapped up

145

in his or her own life as I am in mine. And in these moments, when I get out of the box toward them, other drivers seem very different to me. In a way, I feel that I understand them and can relate to them, even though I know basically nothing about them."

"Yeah," I nodded, "I've had that experience too."

"Good. So you know what I'm talking about. With that kind of experience in mind, let's consider your question. You're worried that in order to stay out of the box you'd have to do everything that pops into your head to do for others. And that seems overwhelming, if not foolhardy. Am I right?"

"Yes. That's one way to put it."

"Well," said Lou, "we need to consider whether being out of the box creates the overwhelming stream of obligations you're worried about. Let's consider the driving situation. First of all, think of the people in the cars far ahead and far behind me. Is my being out of the box likely to make much of a difference in my outward behavior toward *them*?"

"No, I suppose not."

"How about toward drivers who are nearer to me? Would my being out of the box change my outward behavior toward *them*?"

"Probably."

"Okay, how? What might I do differently?"

I thought of seeing my neighbor in my rearview mirror. "Well, you probably wouldn't cut people off as much."

"Okay, good. What else?"

"You'd probably drive more safely, more considerately. And who knows?" I added, thinking of the glare I shot at the man who turned out to be my neighbor, "you might even smile more."

146

"Alright, good enough. Now notice—do these behavioral changes strike you as overwhelming or burdensome?"

"Well, no."

"So, in this case, being out of the box and seeing others as people doesn't mean that I'm suddenly bombarded with burdensome obligations. That's because the basic obligation I have as a person—which is to see others as they are, as people—is satisfied, in many cases, by the fundamental change in my way of being with others that happens when I get out of the box. Does that make sense, Tom?"

"Yeah, I think it does."

"Then let me add one more point." Lou leaned forward and folded his arms on the table. "On occasion, there *are* times when we have specific impressions of additional things we should do for others, particularly toward people we spend more time with—family members, for example, or friends or work associates. We know these people; we have a pretty good sense of their hopes, needs, cares, and fears; and we're more likely to have wronged them. All of this increases the obligation we feel toward them, as well it should.

"Now, as we've been talking about, in order to stay out of the box, it's critical that we honor what our out-of-the-box sensibility tells us we should do for these people. However—and this is important—this doesn't necessarily mean that we end up doing everything we feel would be ideal. For we have our *own* responsibilities and needs that require attention, and it may be that we can't help others as much or as soon as we wish we could. But we do the best we can under the circumstances—and we do that because when we're out of the box, seeing others as people, that's what we want to do."

Lou looked at me steadily. "You've learned about self-justifying images, haven't you?"

147

"Yes."

"Well, then you understand how we live insecurely when we're in the box, desperate to show that we're justified—that we're thoughtful, for example, or worthy or noble. It can feel pretty overwhelming always having to demonstrate our virtue. In fact, when we're feeling overwhelmed, it generally isn't our obligation to others but our in-the-box desperation to prove something about *ourselves* that we find overwhelming. If you look back on your life, I think you'll find that's the case—you've probably felt overwhelmed, overobligated, and overburdened far more often *in* the box than *out*. To begin with, you might compare last night with your family to the nights that came before."

That's true, I thought. *Last night—the first time in a while that I'd actually gone out of my way to do something for Laura and Todd—was the easiest night I'd had in I don't know how long.*

Lou paused for a few moments, and Bud asked, "Does that help with your question, Tom?"

"Yeah. It helps a lot." Then I smiled at Lou. "Thanks."

Lou nodded at me and settled back in his chair, apparently satisfied. He looked past me, out the window. Bud and I waited for him to speak.

"As I sat there those many years ago in that seminar room in Arizona," he said finally, "learning from others just as you've learned here from Bud and Kate, my boxes started to melt away. I felt deep regret at how I'd acted toward the people in my company. And in the moment I felt that regret, I was out of the box toward them.

"The future of Zagrum depended," he continued, "on whether I could *stay* out of the box. But I knew that in order to stay out, there were certain things that I had to do. And fast."

22   *Leadership out of the Box*

"In order to see what I needed to do," Lou said, rising from his chair, "you need to understand what the nature of my self-betrayal was." He began to pace the length of the table. "There were many self-betrayals, I suppose, but I realized as I pondered the implications of what I learned in Arizona that I'd betrayed myself at work in one major way. And what we've discovered in the years since is that almost everyone at work betrays himself or herself in this same foundational way. So everything we do here is designed to help our people avoid that self-betrayal and stay out of the box. Our success in *that* endeavor has been the key to our success in the marketplace."

"So what is it?" I asked.

"Well, let me ask you this," Lou said. "What's the purpose of our efforts at work?"

"To achieve results together," I answered.

Lou stopped. "Excellent," he said, apparently impressed.

"Actually, Bud talked about that yesterday," I said, slightly sheepish.

"Oh, did you already talk about the foundational workplace self-betrayal?" he asked, looking at Bud.

"No. We touched on how in the box we can't truly focus on results because we're so busy focusing on ourselves," Bud said, "but we didn't get specific about it."

"Okay," Lou responded. "Well then, Tom, you've been with us now for what—a month or so?"

"Yes, just over a month."

"Tell me about how you came to join Zagrum."

I then related to Lou and Bud my career highlights at Tetrix, my longtime admiration of Zagrum, and the details of my interviewing process.

"Tell me how you felt when you were offered the job."

"Oh, I was ecstatic."

"The day before you started, did you have good feelings about your soon-to-be coworkers?" Lou asked.

"Oh, sure," I answered. "I was excited to get started."

"Did you feel that you wanted to be helpful to them?"

"Yes, absolutely."

"And as you thought about what you would do at Zagrum and how you would *be* on the job, what was your vision?"

"Well, I saw myself working hard, doing the best I could to help Zagrum succeed," I answered.

"Okay," Lou said, "so what you're saying is that before you started, you had a sense that you should do your best to help Zagrum and the people who are part of it succeed—or as you said earlier, achieve results."

"Yes," I answered.

Lou walked over to the board. "Is it okay with you, Bud," he said, pointing toward the diagram of Bud's baby-crying story, "if I change this a little?"

"Absolutely. Please, go ahead," Bud said.

Lou then erased and added to the diagram. He backed away, and this is what he had written:

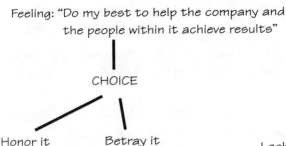

Feeling: "Do my best to help the company and the people within it achieve results"

CHOICE

Honor it   Betray it
                "Self-betrayal"

How I started to see myself	How I started to see coworkers
Victim	Lazy
Hardworking	Inconsiderate
Important	Unappreciative
Fair	Insensitive
Sensitive	Fakers
Good manager	Lousy managers
Good worker	Lousy workers

Lack of commitment
Lack of engagement
Troublemaking
Conflict
Lack of motivation
Stress
Poor teamwork
Backbiting/
  bad attitudes
Misalignment
Lack of trust
Lack of accountability
Communication
  problems

"Notice, Tom," he said. "Most people when they start a job have about the same feelings about it that you did. They're grateful for the employment and for the opportunity. They want to do their best—for their company and for the people in it.

"But interview those same people a year later," he continued, "and their feelings are usually very different. Their feelings toward many of their coworkers frequently resemble the feelings Bud had toward Nancy in the story he told. And you'll often find that people who formerly were committed, engaged, motivated, looking forward to working as a team, and so on, now have problems in many of those areas. And who do you suppose they think *caused* those problems?"

"Everyone else in the company," I answered. "The boss, coworkers, the people who report to them, even the company, for that matter."

"Yes. But now we know better," he said. "When we blame, we blame because of ourselves, not because of others."

"But is that always the case?" I asked. "I mean, when I was at Tetrix, my boss was terrible. He created all kinds of trouble. And now I see why—he was deep in the box. He mistreated everyone in the division."

"Yes," Lou said, "and as hard as we work at this here at Zagrum, you're going to run into people who mistreat you here as well. But look at this diagram," he said, pointing at the board. "Is this worker blaming his coworkers because of what they've done to him, whatever that might be? Or another way to put it is this: Do we get in the box because other people are in *their* boxes? Is that what causes us to get in the box?"

The answer, of course, was no. "No, we get in the box through self-betrayal. I understand that. But I guess my question is, Isn't it possible to blame without being in the box?"

Lou looked at me intently. "Do you have a specific example that we could think about?"

"Well, sure," I said, "I'm still thinking about my old boss at Tetrix. I guess I've been blaming him for a long time. But my point is, he really *is* a jerk. He's a big problem."

"Well, let's think about that," Lou said. "Do you suppose it's possible to recognize how someone might be a big problem without being in the box and blaming them?"

"Yeah, I guess so," I answered. "But if I'm blaming, am I necessarily in the box?"

"Well, you might think about it this way," Lou continued. "Does your blame help the other person get better?"

I suddenly felt quite exposed, as if a lie was about to become public knowledge.

"No, it probably wouldn't," I said.

"Probably?" Lou asked.

"Well, no. I mean, no, my blame wouldn't help the other person get better."

"In fact," Lou continued, "wouldn't blaming provoke that person to be even *worse*?"

"Well, yes, I guess it would," I said.

"Well then, is that blame serving some other useful purpose toward helping the company and those in it achieve results? Is there some out-of-the-box purpose that is served by blame?"

I didn't know what to say. The truth was there *was* no out-of-the-box purpose for my blame. I knew that. I'd been in the box toward Chuck for years. My question to Lou was just a way for me to feel justified in my blame. But my need for justification exposed my self-betrayal. Lou had brought me face-to-face with my lie.

"I guess not," I said.

Bud spoke up. "I know what you're thinking about, Tom. You've had the misfortune of working with someone who was often in the box. And it was a tough experience. But notice, in that kind of a situation, it's quite easy for me to get in the box too because the justification is so easy—the other guy's a jerk! But remember, once I get in the box in response, I actually *need* the other guy to keep being a jerk so that I'll remain justified in blaming him for being a jerk. And I don't need to do anything more than get in the box toward him to keep inviting him to be that way. My blame keeps inviting the very thing I'm blaming him for. Because in the box, I need problems.

"Isn't it far better," he continued, "to be able to recognize others' boxes without blaming them for being in the box? After all, I know what it's like to be in the box because I'm there some of the time too. Out of the box I *understand* what it's like to be in the box. And since when I'm out of the box I neither need nor provoke others to be jerks, I can actually ease, rather than exacerbate, tough situations.

"There's another lesson here, of course," he continued. "You can see how damaging an in-the-box leader can be. He or she makes it all too easy for others to revert to their boxes as well. The lesson, then, is that you need to be a different kind of leader. That's your obligation as a leader. When you're in the box, people follow you, if at all, only through force or threat of force. But that's not leadership. That's coercion. The leaders people *choose* to follow are the leaders who are out of the box. Just look back on your life and you'll see that that's so."

Chuck Staehli's face melted from my mind and I saw Amos Page, my first boss at Tetrix. I would have done anything for Amos. He was tough, demanding, and about as out of the box as I could imagine a person being. His enthusiasm for his work and the industry set the course for my whole career. It had been a long time since I'd seen Amos. I made a mental note to look him up and see how he was doing.

"So your success as a leader, Tom, depends on being free of self-betrayal. Only then do you invite others to be free of self-betrayal themselves. Only then are you *creating* leaders yourself—coworkers whom people will respond to, trust, and want to work with. You owe it to your people to be out of the box for them. You owe it to *Zagrum* to be out of the box for them."

Bud stood up. "Let me give you an example of the kind of leader we need you to be," he said. "My first project as a new attorney was to become an expert in California mobile home law. The results of my research would be crucial to one of the firm's largest clients, for that client's expansion plans required the acquisition of large areas of land then occupied by mobile home parks.

"My supervising attorney on the project was a fourth-year attorney named Anita Carlo. As a fourth-year, she was three years away from partnership consideration. First-year attorneys can afford a few mistakes, but fourth-year attorneys don't have that luxury. By then they're supposed to be seasoned, trustworthy, and competent. Any mistakes at that point in one's law firm life generally count as heavy negatives when it's time for the partnership vote.

"Well, I threw myself into the project. Over the period of a week or so, I probably became the world's foremost expert on California mobile home law. Yippee, right? Well, I laid everything out in a hefty memo. Anita and the lead partner on the project were happy because the result turned out to be good for our client. Everything was good. I was a hero.

"About two weeks later, Anita and I were working together in her office. Almost in passing she said, 'Oh, by the way, I've been meaning to ask you this: Did you check the pocket parts in all the books you used in your mobile home research?'"

I wasn't familiar with the term Bud had just used. "Pocket parts?" I asked.

"Yeah — have you ever been in a law library?"

"Yes."

"Then you know how thick legal books are," he said.

"Uh-huh."

"Well, thick legal books present a printing challenge that is solved by what are called 'pocket parts.' Let me explain. Legal books are in constant need of revision to reflect the latest developments in the law. In order to avoid frequent reprints of very expensive books, most legal reference books include a pocket in the back where monthly updates are stored."

"So Anita was wondering whether you had checked the most up-to-date versions of the law when you made your analysis," I said.

"Exactly. And when she asked the question, I wanted to run and hide because in my exuberance, I never thought to check the pockets.

"Well, we ran up to the firm's law library and began pulling all the books I'd used. And guess what? The law had changed. Not just in a marginal way but in a way that changed everything. I had the client running headlong into a public relations and legal nightmare."

"You're kidding," I said.

"Afraid not. Anita and I went back down to her office to give the bad news to Jerry, the lead partner on the project. He was located in a different city, so we had to call him. Now think about it, Tom," he said. "If you were Anita Carlo, under scrutiny for partnership, what would you have told Jerry?"

"Oh, that this first-year guy messed up or something like that," I said. "I would've found *some* way to make sure that he knew it wasn't my fault."

"Me too. But that's not what she did. She said, 'Jerry, you remember that expansion analysis? Well, I made a mistake on it. It turns out that the law has just recently changed, and I missed it. Our expansion strategy is wrong.'

"I was dumfounded listening to her. *I* was the one who'd messed up, not Anita, but she—with much at stake—was taking responsibility for the error. Not even one comment in her conversation pointed to me.

"'What do you mean *you* made a mistake?' I asked her after she hung up. '*I* was the one who didn't check the pocket parts.' This was her response: 'It's true you should've checked them. But I'm your first supervisor, and a number of times during the process I thought that I should remind you to check the pockets, but I never got around to asking until today. If I had asked when I felt I should've, none of this ever would've happened. So you made a mistake, yes. But so did I.'"

"Now think about it," Bud continued. "Could Anita have blamed me?"

"Absolutely."

"And she would've been justified in blaming me, wouldn't she?" Bud asked. "Because, after all, I really *did* make a mistake. I *was* blameworthy."

"Yeah, I guess that's right," I said.

"But notice," Bud said with feeling, "she didn't *need* to blame me—even though I made a mistake—because she herself wasn't in the box. Out of the box she had no need for justification."

Bud paused for a moment and sat back down. "And here's the interesting thing: Do you suppose that by claiming responsibility for her mistake Anita made me feel less or more responsible for my own?"

"Oh, more," I said.

"That's right," Bud agreed. "A hundred times more. By refusing to look for justification for her relatively little mistake, she invited me to take responsibility for my own major one. From that moment on, I would've gone through a brick wall for Anita Carlo.

"But think how that would've changed," he continued, "if she *had* blamed me. How do you suppose I would've reacted had Anita blamed me when she talked to Jerry?"

"Well, I don't know what you might've done *exactly*, but you probably would've started to find some weaknesses in her that make her hard to work for, for one thing."

"Exactly. And both Anita and I would've then been focused on ourselves instead of what we needed to focus on at that point more than ever—the result for the client."

"And that," Lou said, joining back in, "is exactly what I realized my problem was as I sat in Arizona learning this material. I had failed, in all kinds of ways, to do my best to help Zagrum and its employees achieve results. In other words," he said, pointing to the board, "I'd betrayed my sense of what I needed to do for others in the venture. And in doing that, I buried myself in the box. I wasn't focused on results at all; I was just focused on myself. And as a result of that self-betrayal, I blamed others for everything. That picture there," he said, pointing again at the diagram, "that was me. I saw everyone in the company as problems and saw myself as the victim of their incompetence.

"But in that moment of realization—a moment that one would expect would be dark and depressing—in that moment I felt the first happiness and hope about my company that I'd had in months. Still very unsure of where this would end up, I had an overwhelming feeling of something—a first thing—that I needed to do. Something that I had to do if I was to move forward out of the box.

"I had to go see Kate."

23 Birth of a Leader

"We left Arizona the following night on the red-eye. We'd planned to spend a few days of R&R in San Diego before going home, but our plans had all changed. I'd heard that Kate would be starting her new job in the Bay Area in just a few days. I desperately hoped that I could catch her before she left. I needed to deliver something to her," Lou said, looking past me out the window again. "I needed to take her a ladder."

"A ladder?" I asked.

"Yes, a ladder. One of the last things I did to Kate before she left," he continued, "was demand that a ladder be removed from her sales area. Her department had decided to use the ladder as a visual aid in promoting some sales goals. I thought it was a stupid idea and told her so when she asked me about it. But they went ahead and did it anyway. Later that night, I told the custodial staff to remove the ladder from the premises. Three days later, she and the other four members of the March Meltdown group gave me their two-month's notices. I had them removed by our security staff within an hour—didn't even allow them to go back into their offices alone. *Anyone who turned on me like that couldn't be trusted,* I told myself. And that was the last time I had seen or spoken with Kate.

"I can't explain it, but I just knew that I needed to take her a ladder. It was a symbol of so much. And so I did.

"Carol and I arrived back at JFK at about 6:00 A.M. on Sunday morning. I had the limo driver drop Carol off at home and then take me by the office, where I rummaged through a half-dozen or so supply closets before I found a ladder. We then tied it to the top of the car and headed up to Kate's place in Litchfield. It was about 9:30 or so when I rang her doorbell, the ladder laid across my back.

"The door opened and I saw Kate, her eyes in wide surprise at the sight of me. 'Now before you say anything, Kate, I have something I've got to say, even though I don't know how I can ever begin to say it. First of all, I'm sorry for just barging in on you on a Sunday morning, but it couldn't wait. I . . . umm, I . . . '

"All of a sudden, Kate just busted up laughing. 'Sorry, Lou,' she said, doubled over against the door jamb. 'I know you must have something serious to say, or you wouldn't be here, but the sight of you hunched over with that ladder is just too much to take. Here, let me help you put it down.'

"'Yeah, about the ladder,' I said, 'that's as good a place to start as any. I never should've done what I did. I don't know why I did it, to be honest. I shouldn't have even cared.'

"Kate had stopped laughing then and was listening intently. 'Look, Kate,' I said, 'I've been a real jackass. You know that. Everyone knows it. But I didn't know it until two days ago. Or I couldn't see it, anyway. But I can sure see it now. And the sight of what I've done to the people I care about most in my life terrifies me—and that includes you.'

"She just stood there, listening. I couldn't tell what she was thinking.

"'I know that you've got something really good lined up,' I continued. 'And I'd never expect you to come back to Zagrum—not after the way I've been. But I'm here to plead with you. There's something I've got to talk to you about, and then, if you tell me to, I'll leave and never bother you again. But I see what I've done to mess this all up for everybody, and

I think I have an idea of how to put it back together. I've got to talk to you.'

"She stepped back from the door. 'Okay,' she said. 'I'll listen.'

"Over the next three hours I tried my best to share with her what I'd learned about the box and everything else over the prior couple of days. I think I butchered it pretty badly too," Lou said, looking at me with a smile. "But it wasn't so important what I said. She could tell, whatever it was I was talking about, that I meant it.

"Finally she said, 'Okay, Lou. But I have a question: If I were to come back, how would I know that this isn't just some temporary change? Why should I take the chance?'

"I think my shoulders hunched a bit. I didn't know what to say. 'That's a good question,' I said finally. 'I wish I could tell you not to worry. But I know myself better than that. And so do you. That's one of the things that I want to talk to you about. I need your help.'

"I then explained to her a rudimentary plan. 'Two things need to happen,' I told her. 'First, we need to institute a process in our company where we help people to see how they're in the box and are therefore not focusing on results. Second—and this is key, especially for me personally—we need to institute a system of focusing on results that keeps us *out of* the box much more than we have been: a way of thinking, a way of measuring, a way of reporting, a way of working. For once we're out of the box,' I told her, 'there are a lot of things we can do to help keep us out while going forward. We need to institute such a system at Zagrum.'

"'Do you have some ideas about that?' she asked.

"'Yes. A few, but I need your help, Kate,' I said. 'Together we could figure out the best way to do it. No one I know would be able to do it as well as you could.'

"She sat there in thought.

"'I'm not sure,' she said, slowly. 'I'm going to have to think about it. Can I call you?'

"'Absolutely. I'll be waiting by the phone.'"

24   *Another Chance*

"As you can gather," Lou continued, "she called. I was given a second chance. And the Zagrum you've been admiring over these many years has been the result of that second chance.

"We made a lot of mistakes as we got restarted together. The only thing we did really well to begin with was cover with our people the ideas you've now learned over these last two days. We didn't necessarily know all the implications in the workplace, so at first we stayed at the level of the general ideas. And you know something? It made a big difference. Just what Bud's done for you for these two days, that alone, when learned by people in a common enterprise, has a powerful, lasting effect. We know because we've measured the results over time.

"But over these twenty or so years, we've become much more sophisticated in the specific application of the material to business. As we became more out of the box as a company, we were able to identify and develop a specific plan of action that minimizes the basic workplace self-betrayal that we've been talking about. Right out of the chute, when people generally are still out of the box toward their coworkers and the company, we introduce our people to this way of working together."

Lou paused, and Bud jumped in. "Our effort now is in three phases," he said. "Yesterday and today, you've begun what we call our Phase 1 curriculum. It's all we had in the beginning, and it alone has tremendous impact. It's the foundation for everything that comes later. It's what makes our results here possible. Our work in Phases 2 and 3 will build on what we've covered by plugging you in to a concrete and systematic way of focusing on and accomplishing results—a 'results system' that minimizes self-betrayal at work and maximizes the company's bottom line. And it does this in a way that greatly reduces common organizational people problems. But you're not quite ready for Phase 2 yet."

"I'm not?"

"No. Because although you now understand what the foundational self-betrayal at work is, you don't yet understand the extent to which you are in it. You don't yet understand the extent to which you've been failing to focus on results."

I felt my face begin to slacken again, and I realized in that moment that I hadn't felt that defensive sensation since the morning before. The thought seemed to rescue me, and I returned again to openness.

"But you're no different from anyone else on that score," Bud continued, with a warm smile. "You'll see it soon enough. In fact, I have some material for you to read, and then I'd like to meet with you again in about a week. We'll need about an hour."

"Okay. I'll look forward to it," I said.

"And then the work will begin," Bud added. "You'll need to rethink your work, learn to measure things you never knew needed measuring, and help and report to people in ways you've never thought of. As your manager, I'll help you do all this. And you, as a manager, will learn how to help your people do the same."

Bud stood up. "All of this together makes Zagrum what it is, Tom. We're glad you're a part of it. By the way, in addition to your reading, I have some homework for you."

"Okay," I said, wondering what it might be.

"I want you to think of your time working with Chuck Staehli."

"Staehli?" I asked, surprised.

"Yes. I want you to think about how and whether you really focused on results during the time you worked with him. I want you to consider whether you were open or closed to correction, whether you actively sought to learn and enthusiastically taught when you could have. Whether you held yourself fully accountable in your work, whether you took or shifted responsibility when things went wrong. Whether you moved quickly to solutions or instead found perverse value in problems. Whether you earned in those around you—including Chuck Staehli—their trust.

"And as you think about that, I want you to keep continually in your mind the ideas we've covered. But I want you to do it in a particular kind of way." Bud pulled something from his briefcase. "A little knowledge can be a dangerous thing, Tom. You can use this material to blame just as well as you can use anything else. Merely *knowing* the material doesn't get you out of the box. *Living* it does. And we're not living it if we're using it to diagnose others. Rather, we're living it when we're using it to learn how we can be more helpful to others—even to others like Chuck Staehli.

"Here are some things to keep in mind while you're trying to do just that," he continued, handing me a card.

I looked at it, and this is what it said:

Knowing the material

- Self-betrayal leads to self-deception and "the box."
- When you're in the box, you can't focus on results.

- Your influence and success will depend on being out of the box.
- You get out of the box as you cease resisting other people.

Living the material

- Don't try to be perfect. Do try to be better.
- Don't use the vocabulary—"the box," and so on—with people who don't already know it. Do use the principles in your own life.
- Don't look for others' boxes. Do look for your own.
- Don't accuse others of being in the box. Do try to stay out of the box yourself.
- Don't give up on yourself when you discover you've been in the box. Do keep trying.
- Don't deny you've been in the box when you have been. Do apologize, then just keep marching forward, trying to be more helpful to others in the future.
- Don't focus on what others are doing wrong. Do focus on what you can do right to help.
- Don't worry whether others are helping you. Do worry whether you are helping others.

"Okay, Bud. This will be helpful. Thanks," I said, slipping the card into my briefcase.

"Sure," Bud said. "And I look forward to seeing you again next week."

I nodded, then stood up and turned to thank Lou.

"Before you go, Tom," said Lou, "I'd like to share one last thing with you."

"Please," I said.

"My boy—Cory—do you remember him?"

"Yeah."

"Well, three months after Carol and I watched him drive away, we rode in that same white Suburban to the remote wilderness that had been Cory's home for those months. We were going out to meet him, to live with him for a few days, and then to bring him home. I don't think I've ever been so nervous.

"I had written him frequently in the weeks he was gone. The program leaders delivered letters to the kids every Tuesday. I had poured my soul out to him in those letters, and slowly, like a young foal taking his first uncertain steps out into a stream, he began to open himself to me.

"I had discovered through those letters a boy I never knew I had. He was full of questions and insights. I marveled at the depth and feeling within his heart. But most especially, there was a peace that sung through his prose that had the effect of calming the heart of a father who feared that he'd driven away a son. Every letter sent, and every letter received, was a source of healing.

"As we covered the last few miles to the rendezvous point, I was overcome with the thought of what almost was—a bitterly divided father and son who almost never knew each other. At the brink of war—a war whose effects might have been felt for generations—we were saved by a miracle.

"Driving around the last dusty hill, I saw some quarter mile away the dirtiest, scraggliest-looking group of kids that I'd ever seen—clothes worn and torn, stringy beards, hair

167

three months past due for clippers. But out of that pack flew a lone boy, a boy whose now lean figure I yet recognized through the dirt and grime. 'Stop the car. Stop the car!' I yelled at the driver. And out I flew to meet my son.

"He reached me in an instant and leapt into my arms, tears cutting paths through the dust on his face. And through the sobs I heard, 'I'll never let you down again, Dad. I'll never let you down again.'"

Lou stopped, choking back the memory of the moment.

"That he should feel that for me," he continued, more slowly, "the one who had let *him* down, melted my heart.

"'And I won't let you down again, either, Son,' I said."

Lou paused, separating himself from his memory, and looked at me with his kindly eyes.

"Tom," he said, putting his hands on my shoulders. "The thing that divides fathers from sons, husbands from wives, neighbors from neighbors—the same thing divides coworkers from coworkers as well. Companies fail for the same reason families do. And why should we be surprised to discover that it's so? For those coworkers I'm resisting are themselves fathers, mothers, sons, daughters, brothers, sisters.

"A family, a company—both are organizations of *people*. That's what we know and live by at Zagrum.

"Just remember," he added. "We won't know who we work and live with—whether it be Bud, Kate, your wife, your son, even someone like Chuck Staehli—until we leave the box and join them."

About THE ARBINGER INSTITUTE

"Arbinger" is the ancient French spelling of the word "harbinger." It means "one that indicates or foreshadows what is to come; a forerunner." ARBINGER is a forerunner, a "harbinger," of change.

The change work of THE ARBINGER INSTITUTE grows out of the development at the heart of the human sciences that is introduced in this book. Led by philosopher Terry Warner, a team of scholars has broken new ground in solving the age-old problem of self-deception, or what was originally called "resistance." The problem is this: How can people simultaneously (1) create their own problems, (2) be unable to see that they are creating their own problems, and yet (3) resist any attempts to help them *stop* creating those problems?

As this book explains, this phenomenon is at the heart of much organizational failure. It is the reason many organizational problems seem so intractable—at their core they are self-deceptions; they *resist* solution.

ARBINGER was founded to translate the team's important work on self-deception—and its solution—into practical effect for individuals, families, and organizations worldwide. ARBINGER's focus on organizations began when a well-known management consultant asked for ARBINGER's help with one of his clients. As a result of ARBINGER's work, that company, which had been languishing in its performance, became the industry's profit leader, eventually doubling and tripling the return on investment of its nearest competitors. Out of the reputation that began to spread after that experience,

ARBINGER began to focus on the organizational implications and applications of the self-deception problem and solution.

Today, ARBINGER is a management training and consulting firm and scholarly consortium that includes people trained in business, law, economics, philosophy, the family, education, and psychology. Together, the members of ARBINGER apply their energies to helping organizations reduce people problems and increase bottom-line results. They do this by helping clients implement ARBINGER's three-phase Results System™. Phase 1 of that system is introduced in this book.

ARBINGER's clients come from a wide range of industries, including telecommunications, aerospace, energy, computer technology, finance, banking, steel, automobile manufacturing, retail sales, health care, education, corrections, advertising, and publishing.

Executives and other leaders from these companies have high praise for ARBINGER's products and services. The following are representative statements made on anonymous review sheets during and after implementation of the ARBINGER Results System: "The clarity and power of ARBINGER's work is incomparable. Stunning." "This is the most comprehensive, workable system I have ever seen." "The ARBINGER program is a tremendous tool. There is no comparison to other programs I have participated in." An executive director of a Forbes 40 company that implemented ARBINGER's program said, "I have been involved in 'change effort' work, nationally and at my company, for the past 15 years. ARBINGER's teaching is the most significant breakthrough I have seen in that time. It is on the absolute cutting edge of management theory and practice."

ARBINGER is led by managing directors Duane Boyce, Jim Ferrell, and Paul Smith. For more information about ARBINGER's publications, products, and services, including information regarding seminars and courses for the general public, please visit www.arbinger.com.

THE ARBINGER INSTITUTE
www.arbinger.com
800-307-9415

Index

A

Accountability, lack of, 108, 109 (figure)

Attitudes, bad, 108, 109 (figure)

B

Backbiting, 108, 109 (figure)

Behavior
  distinction between being in or out of the box deeper than, 45–47, 138
  soft versus hard, 45–47
  two ways to perform any, 35, 45–46, 62, 99, 138
  versus way of seeing others, 31–40, 45

Being. *See* Seeing others, two ways of; Ways of being

Blame
  characteristic of self-betrayal, 77–80
  and communication in the box, 132–33
  and coping with others, 131
  due to being in the box, 152–54
  due to ourselves and not others, 152
  emitted in the box, 91
  and feelings, 77–78

felt beneath veneers of niceness, 27
invites one to stay in the box, 92
invites others to be in the box, 92
justifies one's failure to improve, 106
and leaving while in the box, 131
mutual, by two or more people in the box, 92
need for others to be blameworthy created by, 98–99
no need for, out of the box, 157
and thoughts, 77

Blaming emotions/feelings
  created in self-betrayal, 77–80
  as lies, 78–80
  loss of, in getting out of the box, 143

Blindness
  characteristic of being in the box, 15, 100
  to own motivations in the box, 96, 98

Box. *See also* Self-deception
  blaming feelings created in, 77–80

and organizational chart,
125
proof of one's own inno-
cence in, 101
provoked by leaders with
self-justifying images,
124
and resentment of others'
successes, 107
as two or more people in
the box, 101, 124
Commitment, lack of, 108,
109 (figure)
symptom of self-deception,
111
Communication problems,
108, 109 (figure)
symptom of self-deception,
111
Conflict, 108, 109 (figure)

D
Demotivation
function of the box, 44, 47
Do's and Don'ts, 166

E
Effect on others. *See also*
Influence; Leadership
example of negative, 27–28
example of positive, 21–24
function of being in or out
of the box, 31, 43
function of feelings more
than of outward behav-
ior, 24, 26, 31, 97

function of way of being,
43
Engagement, lack of, 108, 109
(figure)

F
Feelings. *See* Blaming emo-
tions/feelings
Four levels of organizational
performance, 51

G
Germ. *See also* Childbed
fever; Semmelweis, Ignaz;
Vienna General Hospital
cause of people problems
analogous to, 19
cause of self-deception
analogous to, 19–20
leadership killed by, 19
no theory of, in
Semmelweis's day,
18–19
self-betrayal as, that causes
self-deception, 111
spread of, analogous to
what occurs in organiza-
tions, 107

H
Hypocrisy
ability to detect, in management practices, 27

175

other people seen as, in the
box, 34, 35–36, 39, 43,
96–97
Obligations, overwhelming
function of being in the
box, 145–48

P
People. *See also* Seeing others,
two ways of; Ways of being
others seen as, the key to
success, 39
others seen as, out of the
box, 34, 35, 39, 46, 47,
147
People problems, 3
box at the heart of, 62
cause of, analogous to a
germ, 19–20
examples of, 108, 109 (figure)
self-betrayal the cause of,
110, 133
single cause of and solution
for, 20
solution to, 20, 110, 111
unifying theory of, 20, 110
People skills
can be in or out of the box
when implementing,
133
effectiveness of, depends on
something deeper, 29
never primary, 28–29
not the key to getting out of
the box, 133–34
Perfection, 59

Phases 1–3, 163–64
Problem, at the heart of
human sciences, 9, 16. *See
also* Self-deception
Problems
creation of, in the box,
101–102
need for, in the box, 99
Proof
being run over provides, of
others' bad behavior,
100
others' blameworthiness
provides, of one's inno-
cence, 101, 103
Provocation
of others to get in the box,
92–93, 106
of problems we blame oth-
ers for, 100–102, 103
of what we say we don't
like, 95, 130
to stay in the box, 130

R
Resistance
box a metaphor for, to others, 140
provoked by leaders, 29,
124
to possibility that one has a
problem, 15, 16, 103
Results
failure to focus on, in the
box, 105–106, 158, 161,
165 (list)
focusing on, 51

177

lack of focus on, 3
need of system for, to stay
out of the box, 161
purpose of work, 104, 149
Results system, 164

S
Seeing others, two ways of,
32–34, 35. *See also*
Objects; People; Ways of
being
function of being in or out
of the box, 34–36
identical to two ways of
being, 35, 60
people or objects, 34–36,
39
and seeing straightfor-
wardly, 34, 35, 39
Self-betrayal, 51, 65–66 (figure), 81. *See also* Box; Self-
deception
blaming character of,
77–80
blaming feelings created in,
77–80
blaming feelings in, as lies,
80
blaming thoughts in, 77–78
cause of being in the
box/self-deception, 51,
75, 76, 111, 152, 165
(list)
examples of, 64, 65, 66
foundational, in the workplace, 111, 149

as germ, 111
key characteristics of,
72–78, 79 (figure)
mutual, as collusion, 101
others' faults inflated in, 76,
79 (figure)
own virtue inflated in, 76,
79 (figure)
self-justifying images in,
82–89, 91–92
self-justifying thoughts and
feelings in, 70–71
self-justifying values
inflated in, 77, 79 (fig-
ure)
and solution to people
problems, 110
view of reality distorted in,
74–75, 81
Self-deception. *See also* Box;
Self-betrayal
cause of, analogous to a
germ, 20
cause of, a unifying theory
of people problems, 20
childbed fever analogous
to, 111
commonness of, in organi-
zations, 15, 16
as disease in organizations,
19–20
effectiveness of people
skills affected by, 29–31
examples of, 10–15, 15–16
and insistent blindness, 15